AWESOME GOD

Songs of His Power

Volume 2

Kevin Straub

World rights reserved. This book or any portion thereof may not be copied or reproduced in any form or manner whatever, except as provided by law, without the written permission of the publisher, except by a reviewer who may quote brief passages in a review.

The author assumes full responsibility for the accuracy of all facts and quotations as cited in this book. The opinions expressed in this book are the author's personal views and interpretations, and do not necessarily reflect those of the publisher.

This book is provided with the understanding that the publisher is not engaged in giving spiritual, legal, medical, or other professional advice. If authoritative advice is needed, the reader should seek the counsel of a competent professional.

Copyright © 2024 Kevin Straub for 4th Angel Publications
Copyright © 2024 TEACH Services, Inc.
ISBN-13: 978-1-4796-1474-5 (Paperback)
ISBN-13: 978-1-4796-1475-2 (ePub)
Library of Congress Control Number: 2021915282

All Scripture quotations, unless otherwise noted, are taken from the KING JAMES VERSION (KJV). Public domain.

Scripture quotations marked NIV are taken from *The Holy Bible*, New International Version®, NIV® Copyright ©1973, 1978, 1984, 2011 by Biblica, Inc.™ Used by permission. All rights reserved worldwide.

Scripture quotations marked YLT are from Young, Robert. *Young's Literal Translation*, 1862. Public domain.

Scripture quotations marked AMPC are taken from the Amplified® Bible Classic, Copyright ©1954, 1958, 1962, 1964, 1965, 1987 by the Lockman Foundation. Used by permission (www.Lockman.org).

The author assumes full responsibility for the accuracy and interpretation of the Ellen White quotations cited in this book.

Published by

TEACH Services, Inc.
P U B L I S H I N G
www.TEACHServices.com • (800) 367-1844

Table of Contents

Introduction—God's People Play a Part in Restoring the Truth about God. 5

Chapter 1—Five Hermeneutic Principles to Apply to the Study of God's Character. 8

Chapter 2—A Herd of Elephants (In the Room of the Hybrid View). 22

Chapter 3—Might Versus Right: A. T. Jones Establishes the Correct Understanding of the Character of God and His Governing Principles 30

Chapter 4—The Christian's Involvement in Human Governments and the Politics of War. 37

Chapter 5—The True Spiritualism: A God of Force. 48

Chapter 6—The Angel, the Sword, and the Tree. 72

Chapter 7—The Korah Rebellion: Destroyed of the Destroyer 90

Chapter 8—The Babel Rebellion: When God Came Down to See 107

Chapter 9—Abraham, Take Now Thy Son 137

Chapter 10—Jesus Invades Jericho, Demolishes Walls, Thousands Killed. 147

Chapter 11—Vengeance Is the Lord's: The Samson Debacle—Homicidal Maniac or Icon of Faith? 163

Chapter 12—Elijah, Elisha, and the Character of God 180

Bibliography *194*

INTRODUCTION

God's People Play a Part in Restoring the Truth about God

"The LORD hath made bare his holy arm in the eyes of all the nations; and all the ends of the earth shall see the salvation of our God."
Isa. 52:10

The introduction to volume 1 of *Awesome God* talks about God's arm and the "dirty power" concept, referring to the common misperception that God uses His direct power to punish and destroy sinners. This is reflected in the cover art for that volume, as well as in the Bible language, as in Isa. 30:30, depicting "the lighting down of His arm" with anger and imagery of destructive elements in nature. As we dig into the truth about God's use of power, we find that it is when He withdraws power that destruction occurs, for His power is ever used only to create, sustain, and protect all that He has made. The Bible uses the language of hot wrath and destruction, while it also provides the keys to interpret that language as what happens when He departs, as in the oft-cited Deut. 31:16-18, that speaks of the hiding of His face when He is rejected for the pursuit of other gods, in whom is no help.

Now that we understand it clearly, we provide the clean image and plain language. This is the last work of the reformation and the core of the loud cry in the closing up of the great controversy. Again, we turn to the prophet Isaiah, who speaks of the people that know the character (name) of God. The final generation watchmen of the Lord will publish the truth about God, lifting up their voices, singing of His power to save.

> Therefore **my people shall know my name**: therefore [they shall know] in that day that I [am] he that doth speak: behold, [it is] I.
>
> How beautiful upon the mountains are the feet of him that bringeth good tidings, that publisheth peace; that bringeth good tidings of good, that publisheth salvation; that saith unto Zion, Thy God reigneth!
>
> Thy **watchmen shall lift up the voice**; with the voice together **shall they sing: for they shall see eye to eye**, when the LORD shall bring again Zion.
>
> Break forth into joy, **sing together**, ye waste places of Jerusalem: for the LORD hath comforted his people, he hath redeemed Jerusalem.
>
> **The LORD hath made bare his holy arm in the eyes of all the nations**; and all the ends of the earth shall see the salvation of our God.
>
> Depart ye, depart ye, go ye out from thence, touch no unclean [thing]; go ye out of the midst of her; **be ye clean, that bear the vessels of the LORD** (Isa. 52:6-11, emphasis added).

So, we can see the imagery of cleanliness in the people that bear the message. They will understand aright and will teach others to look upon a clean picture of the power of God, as represented by His arm. They sing a new song with a new understanding, not as the awesome destructive power of God, but of the awesome power of God to save. They will understand and teach that God is not bringing fire to destroy, but the fire He brings is Himself, desiring that we be in harmony with Him, that we might live in peace and righteousness, for to be out of phase with the light of His presence and love is to be undone.

At this point, readers will understand the principles by which destruction of sinners takes place and be prepared to delve into some more difficult Bible stories in exploration of what is really going on behind the language. It is our prayer that the studies in these volumes will serve to equip the saints to sing the new song and, with the prophet Isaiah, "make bare his holy arm in the eyes of all the nations," as the end of Satan's kingdom draws near, when the principles of force and deception are on display for all to see the contrasting governments of evil and righteousness.

CHAPTER 1

Five Hermeneutic Principles to Apply to the Study of God's Character

"And it is necessary now that the minds of God's people should be opened to understand the Scriptures.
To say that a passage means just this and nothing more, that you must not attach any broader meaning to the words of Christ than we have in the past, is saying that which is not actuated by the Spirit of God ….
The truth, as it is in Jesus, is capable of constant expansion, of new development, and like its divine Author it will become more precious and beautiful; it will constantly reveal deeper significance, and lead the soul to aspire for more perfect conformity to its exalted standard."
"Danger in Rejecting Light," *The Review and Herald*, October 21, 1890, par. 1.

Oftentimes when we raise points of discussion about God's character, focusing upon His love and goodness and declaring, along with John, that He is all light and no darkness in Him, there will be those eager to remind us that we must also not forget that He is also a God of justice. The thinking behind this warning is that sinners should be afraid of what

God will do to them nor should the saints become complacent, for God can and does come to a point where He punishes the rejecter of His mercy by actively bringing about death and destruction, sometimes by very painful and cruel means.

It is our position that words such as *"justice," "punish," "recompense,"* etc., when applied to the Creator, must be defined carefully, within their context. We must not fall into the trap of creating God in our own image. Many tend to believe being created in His image includes our emotional makeup in its fallen state, thereby representing His anger after the manner of our own anger. The Scriptures obviously state repeatedly that God possesses wrath and anger and that He is an administrator of vengeance and justice, but never do they say that we as carnal humanity can liken our emotional states and passions, or our systems of law and order, to the Divine mind and character. In fact, we are informed to the contrary. The bottom line is that what we are in the natural state is not derived from God, nor is what He is as divinity in any way derived from us nor should His character be likened to ours.

Bible students are familiar with the biblical description of how God thinks and operates, in contrast to how man thinks and operates. These are vastly diverse, "as the heavens are higher than the earth" (Isa. 55:9). Note that this statement is within the context of the promise of God's mercy and forgiveness (Isa. 55:7). Man's ideas of righteousness and justice are in opposition to God's mercy and forgiveness. In human systems, when "justice is served," there is the application of a penal code. Absorbing the cost to self and others while freeing the guilty is not man's way.

We read many times in the Scriptures that His mercy endures forever, so whatever path we take to interpret the biblical language of His wrath must follow consistently alongside this picture of the eternal mercy and forgiveness of God to prevent from ending up in the dark forest.

It is extremely rare to find "restorative justice" in modern judicial systems that are primarily focused on a crime, a lawbreaker, and a punishment. Restorative programs exist, but only on the margins of the judicial system or in special cases of history, such as the Truth and Reconciliation

Commission program (South African Truth and Reconciliation Commission, https://1ref.us/stra1 [accessed July 31, 2021], which began hearings in 1996 after the abolition of apartheid in South Africa. It is interesting to note that, according to a University of Pennsylvania study in 2007, it was found that restorative justice is effective in reducing recidivism ("Community Health & Restorative Practices, Reports and Recommendations," International Institute for Restorative Practices, https://1ref.us/stra2 [accessed Dec. 7, 2022]). In an overwhelming majority of cases, however, the many systems of imposed and arbitrary laws, rules, and regulations that are devised by humans carry along with them penalties and punishments for infractions, which are themselves also imposed and arbitrary. Penalties are decided upon and carried out by those who are vested with the power and authority to do so. They are thought up in human minds and codified by human legislative bodies as legally binding in the governance of humanity, by humanity, and for humanity. That is, until another human or group of humans, with the authority and power to do so, comes along and repudiates or changes the laws and/or the punishments, oftentimes for self-serving interests.

But God does not change (see Mal. 3:6; Heb. 13:8). This is an important characteristic of our Creator, and we do well to fix it indelibly in our minds. When He speaks, whatever it is that He declares or brings about, stands forever (see Ps. 33:9, 11; Isa. 55:11). Reading comparatively between the Old and New Testaments, it may seem that God changes His way of operating but, when we understand the subject of God's "permissive will," we have an entirely new perspective from which to interpret the Scriptures. God always acts according to the same set of principles, never deviating in the slightest. The reason He appears to be changeable is because He makes accommodations in response to man's ignorance and hardness of heart. God, therefore, gives instructions within humanity's faulty paradigm of self-governance, but this does not mean He condones that paradigm. God's involvement with or winking at the human practices of wars, civil punishments, divorce, slavery, or polygamy should never be attributed to any institution of the Divine will, but rather seen as a Divine concession to pitiful humanity trying to survive limited wrath, under a fearful condition of a certain degree of separation, i.e., a partial separation from God. (Total separation would be the cessation of existence.)

So, let's begin with a basic question: Did Jesus repudiate the "eye for an eye" system of law? If He did and that is the case, then those who hold that God stands as a destroyer—in the same sense that man destroys—have a notion of justice that is entirely rooted in man's carnal nature apart from the character of God. If we understand, according to the unabashed use of the biblical term *wrath*—using human wrath as the basis for the definition—it would seem that God is going to inject His life-giving power as the Creator in order to keep the willfully impenitent alive while maintaining the function of nerves and tissues until the sweet release of death, for the purpose of torture (all this is based upon a pre-determined judgment in which the redeemed will participate in sentencing (White, *Early Writings*, pp. 52, 54), wherein the impenitent must suffer varying intensities of pain for varying durations of time according to their works (White, *The Great Controversy*, p. 544), until they finally expire in the fire (White, *Early Writings*, p. 294). A surface and literal reading of these passages in inspiration raises much consternation in many. This is why we have to be careful to obtain keys to interpretation from the text. The key to understanding this "fire that is not quenched" which shall destroy "every unrepentant sinner" is found in paragraph 13 of "Christ and the Law" in *The Signs of the Times* (April 14, 1898, par. 13). This topic is covered in detail in volume 1 of *Awesome God,* in the chapter on the fires.

Note the angst that was aroused by Americans when it was discovered that their government allowed torture, as utilized at the facility at Guantánamo Bay (*Guantánamo Bay: 14 Years of Injustice*). Are Americans who believe that justice is served by various punishments (per the penal code) and that the employment of lethal force in both civil and military applications is justified, actually more humane and righteous than God?

God destroys, but it is according to His character. The Bible language that God was given to work with is Babylonian, in the sense of man's legal systems. God uses our manner of speaking in the realm of wrath and punishment, while being careful to give us His own definition within the pages of inspiration. The principle is found in Deuteronomy 31:17, 18, where, according to the "principle of first mention," His anger is His withdrawal of protections, the hiding of His face. When God "gives over," or "departs," other phrases used in the KJV to depict the same thing, there are four basic powers that are enabled to effect destructive forces. These are listed in this volume, in the chapter about elephants in the room, so I won't repeat them here, except to say that His power keeps a check on the wickedness of living beings and on the chaos of nature. In each case the removal of Divine restraint upon these forces is that which allows them to operate outside of Divine order, turning them into agents of destruction.

The wrath, or anger, of God is also demonstrated when He gives over to unrighteous human desire or self-will. This is called the "permissive will" of God, i.e., the "accommodation" of God to human stubbornness and ignorance. It is seen in instances such as Israel picking up the sword. God never intended for them to do this. He never intended for them to see war, which is why He led them out by the wilderness route that He chose for them at the Exodus (Exod. 13:17, 18). We can easily understand that if God had wanted a military paradigm to serve in the conquest of Canaan, He would not have sent Moses for forty years into the wilderness to learn meekness and humility, after his murder of the Egyptian oppressor. "It was not God's will to deliver His people by warfare, as Moses thought" (White, *Patriarchs and Prophets*, p. 247).

In another example, again involving Moses, God's permissive will is seen in Moses' asking for another person to speak in his stead. God, in "anger," gave him Aaron (Exod. 4:10–14). It is seen again in the Israelites' asking for a king. This was against God's counsel, but He gave them a king anyway. Hosea 13:11 says God gave them a king "in mine anger," and verse 9 says they destroyed themselves. Psalm 78:27–31 shows permissive will functioning by the raining of birds upon them in their desire for meat. God "gave them their own desire"—that which would destroy them—by stepping aside and letting them have their way and bearing the result as

"The wrath of God came upon them, and slew the fattest of them, and smote down the chosen men of Israel."

God's dealing with sin and sinners is according to a solitary and undeviating principle. God is unchanging. There is one perfect way to destroy and that is by love, not force.

> Compelling power is found only under Satan's government.
>
> The Lord's principles are not of this order. His authority rests upon goodness, mercy, and love; and the presentation of these principles is the means to be used. God's government is moral, and truth and love are to be the prevailing power. (White, *The Desire of Ages*, p. 759)

We cannot divide up all the destructive acts of God into two columns and apply the labels "God allows these things to happen by themselves" at the head of one column and "God enacted these things Himself" on the other. There is no biblical hermeneutic principle for this.

We must derive our hermeneutics (interpretive principles) from these five sources:

Hermeneutic Principle 1: Common Sense

> The philosophy of common sense is of far more importance ... than the study of Greek and Latin. ("God's Word Our Study-Book," *The Youth's Instructor*, June 30, 1898, par. 7)
>
> We are to be guided by true theology and common sense. (White, *Counsels to Parents, Teachers, and Students*, p. 257)
>
> God wants us all to have common sense, and He wants us to reason from common sense. Circumstances alter conditions. Circumstances change the relation of things. (White, *Manuscript Releases*, Vol. 6, p. 354)

For example, the law says not to kill, and God's character is a transcript of His law. Distinctions between "kill" and "murder" are artificial, as they come from human reason and from human legal codes, not from the Hebrew words. Common sense tells us that *love*, in order to *be love*, must be *free*. That is, it must be free to serve God joyfully by free choice and with all the heart, free from fear. You cannot have a marriage proposal with a .44 on the table nor can you have a connubial relationship with the firearm mounted on the wall above the marriage bed. Virtually everyone understands this. There is no love in that kind of relationship. In that, 1 John 4:18 is clear: "There is no fear in love; but perfect love casteth out fear: **because fear hath torment**" (emphasis added). The New International Version (NIV) says, "because fear has to do with punishment."

> God's dealing with sin and sinners is according to a solitary and undeviating principle. God is unchanging. There is one perfect way to destroy and that is by love, not force.

Logic and common sense have a strong and valid appeal, but the use of these has created many atheists who disavow God because of the darkened views of God foisted upon them by those who claim to represent Him according to a faulty handling of the biblical language. In other words, they say, "If God is a Being Who desires from His subjects a loyal service of love and respect within the context of freedom of choice and non-coercion, yet in the end is the very One who will effect a violent and painful punitive destruction of those who exercise their God-given freedom … well, you people are crazy. Count us out." In this, they reason correctly. God desires us to use our reasoning powers and to understand how He operates to obtain a correct understanding of the language of wrath so we may pass it on to the skeptic who is reading the Bible according to the literal understanding of man's wrath and God's wrath being the same—hot and vengeful.

> All whom God has blessed with reasoning powers are to become intellectual Christians. ("Co-Laborers with Christ," *Review and Herald*, March 8, 1887, par. 1)
>
> Study the character of God. (White, *Counsels to Parents, Teachers, and Students*, p. 402)
>
> There are yet new views of truth to be seen, and much to be understood of the character and attributes of God. (White, *Fundamentals of Christian Education*, 444)

Hermeneutic Principle 2: Inspired Keys

I mentioned one inspired key previously from Deuteronomy. This was the "first mention" definitive. Look at another example, having to do with the flood. In Isaiah 54:7–9, the wrath of God is equated to the hiding of His face and the statement that this is what happened at the flood. God's activity there was only to save. That's why He had Noah make a boat. Again, God's activity at the flood was to use the water to save His people. In 1 Peter 3:20 we read "eight souls were saved by water." There are numerous statements in the Bible that show us God's wrath is in effect when He leaves. "How long, LORD? wilt thou hide thyself for ever? shall thy wrath burn like fire?" (Ps. 89:46). In the Spirit of Prophecy, we have many descriptions of this reality, such as the following examples, noting that punishment comes by His withdrawal from living beings—that their wicked ways may be released—and from nature that it may be given up to chaotic and destructive action. (Nature's forces are given up to chaotic action as opposed to benevolent action. The energetic forces are always there. With God, they are organized to beneficent ends. Without Him they have no control over their energetic forces.)

> Said the angel, "God leaves not His people, even if they err. He **turns not from them in wrath** for any light thing." (White, Letter 17, Dec. 7, 1862, par. 4, emphasis added)

God does not stand toward the sinner as an executioner of the sentence against transgression; but He leaves the rejectors of His mercy to themselves, to reap that which they have sown .... The Spirit of God, persistently resisted, is at last withdrawn from the sinner, and then there is left no power to control the **evil passions of the soul**, and no protection from **the malice and enmity of Satan.** (White, *The Great Controversy*, p. 36, emphasis added)

I was shown that the judgments of God would not come directly out from the Lord upon them, but in this way: They place themselves beyond His protection. He warns, corrects, reproves, and points out the only path of safety; then if those who have been the objects of His special care will follow their own course independent of the Spirit of God, after repeated warnings, if they choose their own way, then He does not commission His angels to prevent **Satan's decided attacks** upon them. (White, *Manuscript Releases*, Vol. 14, p. 3, emphasis added)

Satan works through the elements also to garner his harvest of unprepared souls. He has studied the secrets of the laboratories of nature, and he uses all his power to control the elements as far as God allows. (White, *The Great Controversy*, p. 589, emphasis added)

There will soon be a sudden **change in God's dealings**. The world in its perversity is being visited by casualties,—by floods, storms, fires, earthquakes, famines, wars, and bloodshed. The Lord is slow to anger, and great in power; yet He will not at all acquit the wicked. 'The Lord hath His way in the whirlwind and in the storm, and the clouds are the dust of His feet.' O that men might understand the patience and longsuffering of God! He is **putting under restraint His own attributes. His omnipotent power is under the control of Omnipotence ....** But His forbearance will not always continue. Who is prepared for the sudden change that will take place in God's dealing with sinful men?

Who will be prepared to escape the punishment that will certainly fall upon transgressors? (White, *Fundamentals of Christian Education*, p. 356, emphasis added)

Hermeneutic Principle 3: The Great Controversy Theme

At the beginning of the rebellion, God did not employ His power to eliminate the sinner. Unchanging, neither will He do this in the end. Besides, it is not in His character to use His power in this way. Destruction comes rather when He *removes* His power. But even this He did not do at the beginning because it would have given the impression that He is One Who actively executes "the sentence against transgression" (see White, *The Great Controversy*, p. 36). If God had stepped aside and let the full consequence of rebellion immediately discharge, it would have played into Satan's lies about Him being an arbitrary dictator, making laws that were self-serving. It would have changed the entire economy and fabric of the universe. What God did instead was to let Satan's claim be proven false by exemplification.

The great controversy is not a trial of man, but of God's character and governing system.

Satan was cast out to the earth, whereupon he deceived humanity about the character of God. But God had "the Plan"—the everlasting covenant to give the deceived a way out—a plan to extend a time-out on destruction by imputing justification to all. That is a theological mouthful! More simply stated, He extends a probationary period so that everyone can understand what is happening and make an intelligent choice. By grace and mercy, through Christ, He can, in righteousness, give life to sinners while they demonstrate their full intent to hang on to sin or to be remade in the image of God. Only when these issues are finally made clear—when all participants and onlookers are satisfied that the intent of the impenitent sinner is to not have God in their thinking or actions (when they refuse finally to live by His governing principles of operation in *full recognition* of the fact that these are the only means of entrance into eternal life)—only then does He at last give them over to that choice, which is a cessation from Himself, wherein is the only source of life. The great controversy is not a trial of man, but of God's character and governing system.

> God could have destroyed Satan and his sympathizers as easily as one can cast a pebble to the earth; but He did not do this. **Rebellion was not to be overcome by force. Compelling power is found only under Satan's government. The Lord's principles are not of this order.** His authority rests upon goodness, mercy, and love; and the presentation of these principles is the means to be used. God's government is moral, and truth and love are to be the prevailing power. (White, *The Desire of Ages*, p. 759, emphasis added)
>
> It was God's purpose to place things on an eternal basis of security, and in the councils of heaven it was decided that time must be given for Satan to develop the principles which were the foundation of his system of government. He had claimed that these were superior to God's principles. **Time was given for the working of Satan's principles, that they might be seen by the heavenly universe.** (White, *The Desire of Ages*, p. 759, emphasis added)
>
> In the day of final judgment, every lost soul will understand the nature of his own rejection of truth. The cross will be presented, and its real bearing will be seen by every mind that has been blinded by transgression. Before the vision of Calvary with its mysterious Victim, sinners will stand condemned. Every lying excuse will be swept away. Human apostasy will appear in its heinous character. **Men will see what their choice has been. Every question of truth and error in the long-standing controversy will then have been made plain. In the judgment of the universe, God will stand clear of blame for the existence or continuance of evil.** It will be demonstrated that the divine decrees are not accessory to sin. There was no defect in God's government, no

cause for disaffection. When the thoughts of all hearts shall be revealed, both the loyal and the rebellious will unite in declaring, "Just and true are Thy ways, Thou King of saints. Who shall not fear Thee, O Lord, and glorify Thy name? … for **Thy judgments are made manifest**. Revelation 15:3, 4. (White, *The Desire of Ages*, p. 58, emphasis added)

God forbid: yea, let God be true, but every man a liar; as it is written, That thou mightest be justified in thy sayings, and mightest overcome **when thou art judged.** (Romans 3:4, emphasis added)

Saying with a loud voice, Fear God, and give glory to him; for **the hour of his judgment** is come: and worship him that made heaven, and earth, and the sea, and the fountains of waters. (Revelation 14:7, emphasis added)

Hermeneutic Principle 4: The Bible and Spirit of Prophecy Narratives

We must learn how to decode properly the Bible language to bring harmony to *apparently* conflicting narratives. There are passages and stories that say God Himself did it, compared with other passages that show the mechanism: e.g., Mrs. White says that angels of God destroyed Jerusalem so that one stone was not left upon another. We know from recorded history that the Roman armies under Titus razed the city. The Bible says that God slew Saul. We know from the account that Saul killed himself and that this was the wrath of God (1 Chron. 10:4; cf. 10:14; Hosea 13:11). The Bible says God incited David to take the census (to count fighting men for national security) but, when the curtain is pulled back, we see that God, in the modality of Divine anger, gave David over to Satan, who was the true instigator against David to urge him toward conducting the census (2 Sam. 24:1; cf. 1 Chron. 21:1).[1]

---

[1] The Author has a full presentation of these subjects in a lecture series entitled, "The Bible Says … The Bible Means."

It remains that the burden of proof is upon the proponent of the "destroyer God" to show that God kills as man kills. "For the wrath of man worketh not the righteousness of God," says James 1:20. To say that God uses creative power to make or amass the forces of nature or that He inspires men or angels to do destructive or killing acts would be a revelation of a god who works under carnal principles, according to the wrath of man, which is according to the eye-for-an-eye retributive principle. That is a god created in man's own image, philosophy, and false science. Once we understand how to interpret Divine wrath according to the inspired keys, the biblical narratives that seemed to be in conflict with each other will resolve perfectly.

Hermeneutic Principle 5: Jesus Christ

Jesus never killed or destroyed. We could discuss the cleansing of the temple or the cursing of the fig tree, but those are full studies outside of the scope of this quick overview of interpretive principles. Jesus did not hit anyone, nor threaten to, nor did He kill the fig tree. But let's look at what we can show, in brief, of the things He actually demonstrated that support the truth about God.

The cross itself is "Exhibit A." There it is seen that God lays down His own life rather than kill the sinner. There it is seen that the punishment for sin is "giving over." Jesus did not burn up, even though Lamentations 1:12, 13 says that the LORD afflicted Him in fierce anger from above, sending fire into His bones. Ellen White applies this to Christ ("Christ Our Hope," *Review and Herald*, Dec. 20, 1892, par. 6). The fire of judgment in the Bible is a very interesting subject and we see how it destroys the sinner when we study it carefully. The inspired clarification of it reveals that it is a realization that sin destroys by cutting off the soul from God. "This," she says, "is a fire unquenchable, and by it every unrepentant sinner will be destroyed" ("Christ and the Law," *Signs of the Times*, Apr. 14, 1898, par. 13). The cross reveals the "hiding of His face" principle.

Ellen white says, "How then did God feel when the Son of His love was despised by those whom He came to elevate and ennoble and save? He saw Him dying on the cross, mocked at and jeered at by the passers-by, and He hid as it were His face from Him" ("Knowing Christ," *Signs of the Times*, Jan. 27, 1898, par. 13).

The hiding of His face principle is the same thing as "sparing not," "giving over," "giving up," or "delivering up." God hands the sinner over to outside forces that do the actual destroying. This is the mechanism by which Jesus was destroyed. Romans 8:32 is definitive: "He that spared not his own Son, but delivered him up for us all." Jesus showed us how sinners would die at last. God did not send fire on Him from the sky to burn His flesh while He writhed in sizzling agony, as we think He will do to the impenitent at the end. Please, for God's sake, go look again at what Jesus thought about this idea! When the disciples found themselves rejected by sinners, they looked to Carmel and thought about the fire that Elijah had called upon the military units of fifty men, and they had very definite thoughts about how God functions in wrath. They believed that God sends fire by His own volition and power to destroy His enemies. So they thought that they too should exercise Divine power to bring fire on the heads of those who rejected them as emissaries of God. But *Jesus* said—oh, *what* did He say? You have to get this, you just have to understand it! It will guide you into a precise understanding of God's method of operation. Fix it in your mind—He basically said that God does not operate that way. Satan operates that way. "You don't know what spirit is motivating you. I came not to destroy anyone but to save them."

God's acts are always to save. Destruction comes by men's own choices to turn away from salvation. This does not mean that God must then kill them.

CHAPTER 2

A Herd of Elephants (In the Room of the Hybrid View)

"Jesus Christ the same yesterday, and to day, and for ever."
Heb. 13:8

"I change not; therefore ye sons of Jacob are not consumed."
Mal. 3:6

"Every good gift and every perfect gift is from above, and cometh down from the Father of lights, with whom is no variableness, neither shadow of turning."
James 1:17

Three Views in Adventism on Modality of Divine Wrath		
	Premillennial	Postmillennial
Standard or Traditional View	ACTIVE/PASSIVE	ACTIVE
Hybrid or Maxwellian View	ACTIVE/PASSIVE	PASSIVE
New or Consistent View	PASSIVE	PASSIVE

There are three views in Adventism concerning the modality of Divine wrath. These include the standard or traditional view, the hybrid or

Maxwellian view, and the new or consistent view. These views are divided into two parts: the pre-millennial view and the post-millennial view.

We begin with the "new view" (or the "consistent view") of the wrath of God because it is the correct view by which we shall evaluate the others. The consistent view holds that God does not ever exercise direct violence, and He does not employ physical force to bring about victories in the overall progress of the epic battle we know as "the great controversy," nor in the final showdown around the New Jerusalem, known as the battle of "Gog and Magog" (Ezek. 38:2; Rev. 20:7–8). This view is called "new" because it is a present truth development in the advancement of the reformation of understanding the glory of God which is His righteous character. It is called "consistent" because it holds that God never changes and because it is consistent with the principles of love that are freedom of choice and non-coercion. In the consistent view, all destruction attributed to God is passive. Any time you have such "judgment" or "punishment," it is not God exerting physical power, but rather it is God giving over to outside forces. Neither is this "giving over"—which we might call "Divine recession"—an arbitrary act on God's part, because His withdrawal from the role of Protector and Sustainer is in honor of free will. Decay and death are the natural results of free will exercised in the rejection of God for other gods or for no god. This allowing of the consequences without a saving interference is the justice of God.

The hybrid view or Maxwellian view (as in A. Graham Maxwell's "Larger View," https://1ref.us/strb [accessed August 4, 2021]), which is fashionable doctrine within the domain of institutional Adventism today, teaches that God functions according to the traditional view in Adventism, but only in the premillennial phase. In this middle-of-the-road view, the second death of the finally impenitent, in the postmillennial phase, will be the result of God giving them up in a passive wrath modality.

The standard or traditional view holds to a dual modality in Divine wrath. That is to say, it teaches that God's wrath functions both in an "active" and a "passive" mode. In the premillennial phase, God is seen to work within both modalities, while in the postmillennial phase He only uses "active" wrath. In this view, He is a God who is seen to actively exercise power to do things such as create fire to burn the wicked, directly manipulate the elements for destructive and punitive purposes or, in the case of ancient Israel, give instructions in the use of the sword or other violent means in order to subdue the enemy or correct or punish internal dissension and crime, by proxy.

In the passive mode, we may apply the "hiding of face" principle, where God "gives up" or "gives over" to outside forces of destruction. These can be one or more of the following:

1. Human wickedness (self)
2. Human wickedness (others)
3. Demonic activity
4. Nature

In the active mode, we find God employing His power in a direct and intentional manner, coming toward the object of wrath aggressively and proactively, much as a man would pick up a stick to attack another person.

In the standard view and the hybrid view, we have to admit that it is in God's character to use force and violence, even terrorizing violence and torture, as we would find in the standard teaching on the annihilation of the wicked, where God is believed to sustain their bodies in fire, in many cases for extended periods of time, solely to satisfy "justice" according to a definition that requires an imposed punishment. We find that somehow John's teaching that Jesus came to show us that God is absolute light (life) and in Him is no death (darkness) at all (1 John 1:5; John 1:4, 9) must be interpreted in such a way as to admit that He could actually bring about the first death, as in the hybrid view, or both the first and second deaths, as in the standard view. Also, not only can and does He impose it personally, He is often seen to do it by cruel and unusual means.

The teaching that God functions with two modalities of wrath is lacking in biblical support. There is no hermeneutic principle for it (Straub, "Righteous Evil," in *Awesome God: Songs of His Power, Volume 1*). In other words, there are no keys given in the Bible or the Spirit of Prophecy to give us license to separate incidents of "active" wrath from "passive" wrath or define how we might differentiate between them. On the other hand, we do have keys that have been given to define God's wrath, such as in Deuteronomy 31:16–18 and Isaiah 57:17 in the Bible and in the Spirit of Prophecy (White, *The Great Controversy*, p. 36 and *Manuscript Releases*, Vol. 14, p. 3). (Note that, when holy angels are represented as destroying, it is done by the mechanism of their being given command to stand down in their power to restrain evil forces from destroying, i.e., "He does not commission His angels to prevent Satan's decided attacks upon them" (White, Letter 14, 1883). When God issues a command for holy angels to destroy, it is Him allowing evil angels to do their work. It is all one and the same action; it is "the same destructive power" (White, *The Great Controversy,* p. 614) that is enacted by the combination of holy restraint being withdrawn and demonic force being released—it is the power of evil forces that finally does the destroying.)

But this section is not meant to be a detailed study of the new or consistent view. We are here dealing with the *hybrid* view—which is popular in some Adventist circles today and is held by pastors/teachers such as Tim Jennings, Ty Gibson, David Asscherick, and others—in order to show that this view is also inconsistent. We will do this by highlighting five major issues that the hybrid view must confront. We call them by the popular expression of "an elephant in the room," denoting any item which should be an obvious issue that participants in a discussion are willfully ignoring because it threatens the standard paradigm or status quo and yet, at the same time, precludes an effective resolution to the problem at hand. In the case of the hybrid view, there are five of these "elephants."

Elephant #1: God's use of violence in the first death is not really killing because it is only the "sleep death." He raises them again in the second resurrection.

Incongruence: These folks that God committed to a "dirt nap" come up in the second resurrection to receive the reward of second death. That God would actively close the probation of these individuals is a de facto second death. It matters not that there is a gap of time between their slaying and their resurrection to receive their "reward." For them, it is a fast-forward in time to judgment. In this scenario, probation is apparently proactively closed against them *by God,* with no second chance.

Elephant #2: God's use of violence in the first death is simply "timing them out" to preserve the race. In Old Testament times, this was done to ensure the preservation of a genetic line to bring forth Jesus incarnate. In New Testament times, it was to ensure that God maintained a people through whom He might raise up the 144,000.

Incongruence: This is an arbitrary use of might in order to ensure a win in the great controversy. It neutralizes the claim that the win is achieved through principle alone, without a resort to physical power. It completely negates any claim that God does not "stack the deck" or manipulate the game in some way to favor Himself and cause others to lose. It invalidates the assertion that the contest is about righteousness versus lawlessness. This is because it brings the element of "might" into the picture. If the contest is not about "right versus might" then "might" is admissible. In that case, there is no contest. God would win from the very inception of a challenge to His government. Furthermore, if *"right"* cannot win by standing upon its own merits, needing *"might"* to help it, then it has no claim to "right" as the sole reason to ask for loyalty and worship. It must also admit that physical power is part of the reason why subjects should bow down. In this modality of governance, subjects do not get to see that *right* can stand alone, but that fear and punishment must be a part of the picture. While they may give assent to *right,* they also must admit that *might* is a factor to be reckoned with.

Any jury of peers asked to judge if participants in the contest were pure in their motivation to serve *that* God with love and loyalty *alone* would not be able to ascertain if those persons were serving God free from any thought of fear and punishment (see 1 John 4:18). This is because the creature cannot know the heart and mind of another creature. In order to make that judgment, the jury of peers would have to rely upon the say-so of God alone. But His "say-so" was not enough to prevent the great controversy. "Rebellion was not to be overcome by force .... The Lord's principles are not of this order. His authority rests upon goodness, mercy, and love; and the presentation of these principles is the means to be used" (White, *The Desire of Ages*, p. 759). It had to be demonstrated.

This demonstration must be consistent, from beginning to end. What God refused to do in the beginning, He must also refuse to do in the middle and at the end. God refused to use His might to put down the rebellion in heaven. It must be seen that "the wages of sin is death" (Rom. 6:23), but that He does not pay them. Separation from God is the only thing required to bring about the cessation of existence of the creature, requiring no particular exertion of force on the part of God; He merely needs to honor the choice of the creature to be self-sustaining and quit extending His sustaining power. He simply "unplugs" from the creature who desired no further contact. This is a self-evident truth, for only in God is there life. "God is the fountain of life; and when one chooses the service of sin, he separates from God, and thus cuts himself off from life" (White, *The Desire of Ages*, p. 764).

Elephant #3: God proactively works to "time out"/induce the "sleep death" through direct use/manipulation of various physical elements of nature.

Incongruence: Justice is ever consistent with freedom and mercy. God gives the free moral agent the choice to die by strife, famine, etc. (see Jer. 34:17). God's mercy always stands, but the free moral agent is able to ultimately step entirely outside of it, reaching a place where there is none. For God to be depicted as the initiating cause of punishment and destruction by the use of various methods such as burying alive, drowning, burning, infliction of disease, etc., is to characterize Him not only as arbitrary, but as an *executioner* of the sentence against transgression (which He is not)—by the use of cruel and unusual punishments, the likes of which many, if not most, of the governments of this present world have outlawed for use within their penal systems or even in times of war.

> But when men pass the limits of divine forbearance, that restraint is removed. God does not stand toward the sinner as an executioner of the sentence against transgression; but He leaves the rejectors of His mercy to themselves, to reap that which they have sown. (White, *The Great Controversy*, p. 36)

Even though we may eliminate God's use of personal power in the final destruction of the wicked, to allow that God has acted directly in these voluntary selections of terrible deaths as seen in many Old Testament stories—deaths fraught with terror and torture—is to cast a fearful shadow over His character.

Elephant #4: God uses two modalities of wrath in the premillennial phase, "active" and "passive."

> *Separation from God is the only thing required to bring about the cessation of existence of the creature*

Incongruence: As was also discussed in the introductory remarks, there is no valid hermeneutic principle to establish this proposition. The key to Divine wrath, as given in inspiration, is that wrath is the hiding of God's face, or the "giving over" principle (see Deut. 31:16–18). The Bible language is based on a general view of Deity that is consistent with ancient pagan concepts of an angry God that depict God as the executioner of wrath. God reaches man in a state of darkened understanding. He speaks Babylonian to those infected by Babylonian principles. This language is used in both cases where the actual mechanism of destruction is revealed and where it is not, e.g., the death of Saul or David's numbering of Israel versus Sodom and Gomorrah, the Assyrian decimation, etc. The problem comes when there is a lack of an inspired interpretive principle in either the Bible or Spirit of Prophecy that would validate this dichotomous approach to defining Divine wrath. In other words, there is a principle employed by interpreters that would seem to tacitly assert that, when there is lacking an actual revelation of the mechanism of destruction (no "etiological solution"), they strangely default to a literal and human understanding of wrath as divinely proactive violence. This is eisegetic in nature; it brings human philosophy into the mix—and is therefore a private interpretation.

Elephant #5: God is acting consistently within the principles of love, even in the use of proactive violence.

Incongruence: At the end of the day, the hybrid view demolishes everything it would propose to uphold: that the law is natural, not imposed, and that God is unchanging, nonviolent, ever merciful, nonarbitrary, loving, etc. In order for *love* to *be* love, it must be *free*. That is to say, if punishment comes in any way by the very hand of the Suitor—the One Who proposes and invites the pursued into a relationship based solely on principles of loyalty, freely offered love, and heart appreciation of character—then there is no way to demonstrate to anyone having questions that *the exercise of might and authority generating fear of punishment is not involved in the process of securing the relationship*. It makes gibberish of the great controversy theme, full stop.

CHAPTER 3

Might Versus Right: A. T. Jones Establishes the Correct Understanding of the Character of God and His Governing Principles

"Thou thoughtest that I was altogether such an one as thyself: but I will reprove thee, and set them in order before thine eyes."
Ps. 50:21

I take a risk in bringing forward the work of A. T. Jones, a pivotal figure in Adventism, who is today greatly disparaged in the official opinion of many denominational leaders.

When we undertake to review the work of Jones and/or his contemporary and partner, E. J. Waggoner, as messengers to the Advent people, we are often met with discouraging remarks about these men being apostates. Without going into details of the history about this subject and "the 1888 message," let it suffice to show that inspiration confirmed the message and ministry of these men during the years that the following message was given. Ellen White even travelled and ministered with them in the 1890s.

As if speaking to the attitudes of today, she stated,

> It is quite possible that Elder Jones or Waggoner may be overthrown by the temptations of the enemy; but if they should be, this would not prove that they had had no message from God, or that the work that they had done was all a mistake. But should this happen, how many would take this position, and enter into a fatal delusion .... They walk in blindness as did the Jews. I know that this is the very position many would take if either of these men were to fall. (White, *1888 Materials*, pp. 1044, 1045)

> The Lord in His great mercy sent a most precious message to His people through Elders Waggoner and Jones .... This is the message that God commanded to be given to the world. It is the third angel's message, which is to be proclaimed with a loud voice, and attended with the outpouring of His Spirit in a large measure. (White, *1888 Materials*, p. 1336)

> An unwillingness to yield up preconceived opinions, and to accept this truth, lay at the foundation of a large share of the opposition manifested at Minneapolis against the Lord's message through Brethren Waggoner and Jones. By exciting that opposition, Satan succeeded in shutting away from our people, in a great measure, the special power of the Holy Spirit that God longed to impart to them. The enemy prevented them from obtaining that efficiency which might have been theirs in carrying the truth to the world, as the apostles proclaimed it after the day of Pentecost. The light that is to lighten the whole earth with its glory was resisted, and by the action of our own brethren has been in a great degree kept away from the world. (White, *1888 Materials*, p. 1575)

> The church of God is to shine as a light to the world, but Jesus is the illuminator, and He is represented as moving among His people. No one shines by his own light. The Lord God almighty and the Lamb are the lights thereof. The message given us by A. T. Jones, and E. J. Waggoner is the message of God to the Laodicean church, and woe be unto anyone who professes to believe the truth and yet does not reflect to others the God-given rays. (White, *1888 Materials*, p. 1052)

As we become students of the messages brought by these men, it becomes apparent that the foundation of that which we today call the "character of God message" was laid down at that very time by these first-call messengers (see Matt. 22:3). As we study this history, we will find that the message was effectively subdued and left to molder in the dust for generations, forgotten until second-call messengers were raised up in the 1950s to represent the Laodicean message once again—as it had come to the people in the previous century—that the glory of God might have been established and the great controversy brought to a close.[2]

In the following passages, I have found some of the most decisive testimony to the truths that we are now proclaiming about and by the power of God. I present to you, with joy, the truth about might versus right, as only A. T. Jones could write it! I encourage readers to read the full articles for an additional blessing. This excerpt is from "The Third Angel's Message" by A. T. Jones in the *General Conference Bulletin,* Volume 1, 1895:

> Where did there start in this universe the assumption of any authority or power of might as against right? It originated with the rebellion of Lucifer, in that assumption of self, away back there. He brought that power into this world, and fastened it

---

[2] All of this story is to be found in the author's book *Of the Times and Seasons and the Delay of the Return of Christ* (Aspect Books: Fort Oglethorpe, GA, 2017). The author encourages every reader to obtain and study this book.

upon this world by deception when he got possession of this world. Therefore that word is properly used to show that when God in Christ has lifted us above all the principality and power of this world, it is above this power of might as against right, which is the power of Satan, as he has brought it into this world, and as he uses it in this world. (p. 436)

This simply emphasizes the thought we mentioned a moment ago, that our contest is simply the contest that has been waged from the beginning between the two spiritual powers, between the legal and the illegal powers, between the power of right as against might, and the power of might as against right. The contest is between these two spiritual powers. We have been under the power of might as against right,—the power of force. Jesus Christ brought to us the knowledge of right as against might—the power of love. We forsook the dominion and power of might as against right—the power of force; and have joined our allegiance to the power of right as against might,—the power of love. And now the contest is between these two powers, and concerning us. The contest is always between these spiritual powers. Whatever instruments may be employed in this world as the outward manifestation of that power, the contest is always between the two spiritual powers, Jesus Christ and the fallen prince. (p. 436)

Satan was the one who originated the authority of might as against right. (p. 436)

Now note: The power of right as against might can never use any might. Do you see that? Do you not see that in that lies the very spirit that is called non-resistance of Christians, that is, the very Spirit of Jesus Christ,—which is non-resistance? Could Christ use might in demonstrating the power of right as against might?—No. (p. 437)

To maintain the power of might as against right, might is to be used at every opportunity; because that is the only thing that can be used to win. In that cause the right has only a secondary consideration, if it has any consideration at all. (p. 437)

But on the other hand, the power of right as against might, is in the right, not in the might. The might is *in the right itself*. And **he who is pledged to the principle of right as against might, and in whom that is to be demonstrated, can never appeal to any kind of might**. He can never use any might whatever in defense of the power of right. He depends upon the power of *the right itself* to win, and to conquer all the power of might that may be brought against it. That is the secret. (p. 438, bold emphasis added)

Then don't you see that that explains in a word why it is that Christ was like a lamb in the presence of these powers, and this might that was brought against him? He had nothing to do with using any might in opposing them. When Peter drew the sword, and would defend him he said, Put up your sword: he that taketh the sword shall perish by the sword. (p. 438)

When we get hold of that, all things will be explained as to what we shall do here, there, or the other place. We are pledged to allegiance to the power of right as against might,—the power of love. And Jesus Christ died as a malefactor, abused, tossed about, mobbed, scoffed, spit upon, crowned with thorns, every conceivable contemptible thing put upon him, and he *died under it*, in his appeal to the power of right as against might. And that power of right which he died in allegiance to has moved the world ever since, and it is to move the world in our day as it never has been moved before. **Just as soon as God can get the people who are professedly pledged to the principle, to be pledged in heart to the principle, and put the thought upon nothing at all, and never expect to appeal to anything at all, other than the**

absolute principle of the right and the power of it, to which we are allied, and to which we are pledged, then we shall see, and the world shall see, this power working as never before. (p. 438, emphasis added)

Here is the great issue. Here are the two great powers confronting each other—the Prince of God, Jesus Christ, and the prince of darkness, Satan. Here comes the open conflict. There are but two classes in the world, and every human being will range under one of these two banners—the banner of the prince of darkness or the banner of Jesus Christ. (p. 445)

But to appeal to any kind of might in favor of the right, is to step on which side of the contest? It is instantly to put ourselves on the side of might as against right. And that is the wrong side and that puts us on the wrong side, whatever our profession may be. But to hold steadfastly to the principle of right as against might, right with the might within itself, to win—that is the side of divinity. (p. 445)

Now we will study a little further along that line, in our study of the principle. The power of might as against right, we found in the previous lesson, had taken possession of this world by deceiving and bringing under his power the one into whose possession this world and the dominion of it had been put. Now the Lord, the God of heaven, did not propose to use any of the power of might, any kind of force, to take that dominion out of Satan's hands, even though it be true that he unjustly held it. There would have been no injustice in so taking it back. But that is not God's way of working; that is what we are studying. (p. 446)

I will say this here and can think upon it to all eternity: The universe of God rests upon the principle of self-sacrifice. **The support, the stay of the very universe itself, is the principle of**

sacrificing self to win; that is, to win by nonresistance—to win by the sheer principle of the power of right in itself. That is what holds the universe up. In that it consists. That is simply the gospel. It would be plain enough to say the gospel is that that holds up the universe, but the principle of the gospel is the principle of the sacrifice of Jesus Christ and of God denying Himself and giving Himself in Him. (p. 446, emphasis added.)

So the Lord, in recovering this lost dominion, would not use any might that is not right in itself. Therefore, when He wanted to recover this whole dominion and all of mankind, He went at it in such a way that Satan himself and all of his partisans can never say that it was not fairly done. (pp. 436–446)

The room is silent. Let God be true. Let nothing be said to detract from the might and the right of these words.

CHAPTER 4

The Christian's Involvement in Human Governments and the Politics of War

"The soldiers likewise demanded of him, saying, And what shall we do? And he said unto them, Do violence to no man."
Luke 3:14

"Whereunto," asked Christ, "shall we liken the kingdom of God? or with what comparison shall we compare it?" Mark 4:30. He could not employ the kingdoms of the world as a similitude. In society He found nothing with which to compare it. Earthly kingdoms rule by the ascendancy of physical power; but from Christ's kingdom every carnal weapon, every instrument of coercion, is banished. This kingdom is to uplift and ennoble humanity. God's church is the court of holy life, filled with varied gifts and endowed with the Holy Spirit. The members are to find their happiness in the happiness of those whom they help and bless. (White, *The Acts of the Apostles*, p. 12)

It has been said "that it is difficult to spread the gospel with a Bible in one hand and a missile control switch in the other." This is one of those things that should be self-evident. That Christians should not be involved in military service was a large part of the overall tradition and practice of the first two centuries of Christianity, where "the basic tone was one of polarity between Caesar and the God of the Bible" (Yoder, *Christian Attitudes to War, Peace, and Revolution*, p. 43). Original Christianity, which looks to Christ as its norm, will not engage in politics at any level nor will it be party to the bearing and use of arms.

> The Saviour attempted no civil reforms. He attacked no national abuses, nor condemned the national enemies. He did not interfere with the authority or administration of those in power. He who was our example kept aloof from earthly governments …. Not by the decisions of courts or councils or legislative assemblies, not by the patronage of worldly great men, is the kingdom of Christ established, but by the implanting of Christ's nature in humanity through the work of the Holy Spirit. (White, *The Desire of Ages*, pp. 509, 510)

Original Christianity, which looks to Christ as its norm, will not engage in politics at any level nor will it be party to the bearing and use of arms.

Followers of the biblical Jesus will not be involved in any of the processes pertaining to adjustments of the balances of earthly powers, including voting persons into political office. This is not our work. However, it has come to be standard thinking in Christianity that it *is* a part of our work. The discussions of whether to enter into a war or to stay out of that war are not merely academic in today's Christianity; it is deemed the Christian's *duty* to engage in a politicized Christianity. Today's Christianity, since the time of Constantine, sadly, is not concerned solely with the gospel work. It remains more than an outside observer of the machinations of worldly powers. It is actively seeking to hold positions in the various branches of government, the courts, military service, and law enforcement. Subscribing to the notion of a "just war," Christianity is necessarily fundamentally involved in the geopolitical movements and the questions of taking nation(s) into war or not. If a war should be a "just war," then those Christians will rally to the cause in the munitions factories and send their sons and daughters to die on the field.

Christians would do well to look into their early history to understand how it got that way. The period of the early fourth century saw a "creeping empire loyalty" that led to, what is called by historians, the "Constantinian Shift" (Wikipedia. "Constantinian shift." https://1ref.us/stra3 [accessed August 5, 2021]). This was a drift in the church characterized by an erosion of the standard Christian paradigm of noninvolvement in worldly systems. As Christians changed status from "the persecuted" to "the privileged," it became honorable to serve the state. There developed a duality in the thinking and practice of Christians, which philosophized, "God does some things through the emperor and that God does other things through Christians. God keeps one kind of peace through the emperor and creates other kinds of peace through Christians; the two complement each other" (Yoder, *Christian Attitudes to War, Peace, and Revolution*, pp. 58–59).

There is today a growing understanding among a cross-section of Bible students that embraces this duality, but from an entirely different perspective. Having the wrong perspective leads to tyranny, even "Christian" tyranny. "When that duality is in place ... then Christians are prepared to say that when Caesar converts to Christianity, God will use him as a converted Caesar—not to be a king like Jesus but to be a ruler who favors Christians" (Ibid., p. 59). When we arrive at such a state, we have opened the gate to the development of an imposed version of Christianity and persecution of those who do not subscribe to it. This is nothing less than the career of Rome. A correct biblical perspective will view the worldly systems under Caesar as God's will only in a certain sense, i.e., *permissive will,* which runs counter to His *perfect will.*

The short definition of "permissive will" is when God, in essence, makes concessions for human ignorance and hard-heartedness and—rather than casting His people off to the immediate destruction inherent in their errant philosophies and conduct—He involves Himself in human affairs by counseling and directing in accordance with their own faulty thoughts and ways. All of this is to put a check on a runaway reaction, as coolant slows down a nuclear reaction, preventing an otherwise catastrophic outcome. The Divine intent is to *preserve* and *protect* as much as possible, in order that later generations may come into a fuller understanding of His ways as well as realize the inevitability of the total demise of *anything* that is "given over" by God to function outside of His perfect will. To be clear, this includes everything that operates under the modus operandi of "permissive will" which fails to relinquish its particular idols. Ancient Israel is "Exhibit A" in this matter. They chose the way of the sword. God's "permissive will" gave them laws and instructions governing the use of the sword in both civil and international matters. Yet Jesus later said, "Put away your sword, Peter, for those who live by the sword die by the sword" (see Matt. 26:52). Jesus came speaking directly to clarify God's perfect will as a corrective to that which He allowed under His permissive will. The nation in general refused to relinquish the sword, for they wanted a military Messiah and, when He was not that Man, they killed Him. Then they went on to continue rebelling against the Romans until Jerusalem was destroyed and many were killed in AD 70 (Lohnes, "Siege of Jerusalem: Jewish-Roman War," https://1ref.us/stra4 [accessed Aug. 5, 2021]). We will touch on some of this again in a moment.

What we are getting into has to do with the very core of the great controversy, which is a showcase of contrasting governing systems. God's ways are not like anything on the earth. His government is based upon total other-centered love, which gives all of self for the good of others. There is no concern for self in God's ways, because our needs are satisfied by all the others, who themselves operate under the same system of "all for the other." It is a wonderful trade: *all of self for all of the others*. Satan's operating system is to amass all for self. His way gives benefit to others only if it serves self and sacrifices them as they outlive their usefulness.

God's government is constituted on the twin principles that are the underpinnings of true love: freedom of choice and non-coercion. God does not rule by inducements of reward or threats of punishment. It is preposterous to think that He would represent His overtures of love typically in the marriage relation wherein the suitor, on bended knee proposes his undying loyalty and affection for her to accept or reject. Our proposer is not ever seen to draw his coat aside to reveal a pistol as part of the proposition, nor would he ever carry such a threat into the marriage relation. Yet, we seem to accept without question that God is doing that very thing. He is deemed to hold unconditional love in one hand and the threat of annihilation in the other, should He be refused. Only a despotic man will threaten his wife. Love must be free from threat at the hand of the suitor. It must be free to choose, free from force. The wife of the tyrant husband is not really given a choice. She is being manipulated. Her relationship with her husband is reduced to anxiety, being based on the hope of reward (e.g., she gets to live and hopefully be provided for) and fear of punishment (e.g., he will take her life). There can be no loyalty to such a husband, based upon a heart appreciation of his character and his ways. Only subservience.

So, to bring this around, we find that Christianity today is fundamentally misguided in taking up concerns for the running of this world's systems—systems that are rooted in imposed and arbitrary laws and enforced by threats of arbitrarily imposed violence and/or losses of freedom. Christians can, however, oppose Satan's government without being involved in any politicking and without taking any offices in the governments, militaries, or law enforcement systems of this world—practices that were strictly forbidden in the first centuries of Christianity. When we come to a deeper understanding that it has been Satan's consistent aim "to misrepresent the character of God, the nature of sin, and the real issues at stake in the great controversy" (White, *The Great Controversy*, p. 569) we will be very careful about how we become involved in opposing or supporting political movements or decisions regarding national involvement in the wielding of arms for whatever reasons.

An understanding of the "real issues at stake in the great controversy" (Ibid.) will make us realize that our involvement in the controversy will be through teaching and example, not by serving the political process, nor by careers in enforcement systems that are built upon the deployment and use of deterrents—fines and sanctions, apprehension and detainment systems, and/or lethal weapons. Gun control issues? We should not be involved in the arguments for or against. We know that, in Satan's world, arms are a necessary evil to protect life and property. So, we let the world do as it does. How can we participate in these systems and not have our thinking affected? By beholding we are changed, and much more so by practice. We should be involved only in exposing the principles of Satan's government under which it is deemed necessary for humans to have weapons, as contrasted with God's government which is holy and harmless and undefiled.

"For though we walk in the flesh, we do not war after the flesh: (For the weapons of our warfare are not carnal, but mighty through God to the pulling down of strong holds; Casting down imaginations, and every high thing that exalteth itself against the knowledge of God; bringing into captivity every thought to the obedience of Christ" (2 Cor. 10:3–5).One time when Jesus was out teaching in the countryside, the Roman soldiers came to Him, saying "What shall we do?" He answered them "Do violence to no man" (Luke 3:14). Obviously, this would be a hard saying for a military man or police officer to accept, whose training and employment requires the use of overwhelming force.

We are not to be involved in the world's ways of forcing peace. We understand, according to the modality of God's "permissive will," that these things are necessary. God is represented in the Bible as setting up and tearing down the kingdoms and systems of this world, said to be "His ministers," as it were (Rom. 13:5–6). This is all language that depicts God as doing that which He gives over to. That we live under earthly rulers and powers is part of the curse of sin and not actually a scenario that He ever intended and which He is, in actual fact, working to reverse. Rejecting God means taking other gods and, if other gods are what we want, then the other gods we shall have, according to the fundamentals of God's character and government. As such, the tyranny of man over man is said to be an ordinance of God to which we must submit (Rom. 13:2; 1 Peter 2:13–14). Without any imposed system of law and order, things would run quickly to total destruction, as noted earlier. These systems are not based upon God's ways and, in fact, *they are a part of God's wrath in and of themselves, even while they are necessary to keep in check the escalation of wrath.* Does this make sense? Hosea 13:11 informs us on this point, in that God said, "I gave thee a king in mine anger, and took him away in my wrath." Even the governance of Israel under Moses was expanded to a tiered system of human authority, not because it was God's will, but it was by "permission," a concession that God made:

> The Lord permitted Moses to choose for himself the most faithful and efficient men to share the responsibility with him. Their influence would assist in holding in check the violence of the people, and quelling insurrection; yet serious evils would eventually result from their promotion. They would never have been chosen had Moses manifested faith corresponding to the evidences he had witnessed of God's power and goodness .... Had he relied fully upon God, the Lord would have guided him continually and would have given him strength for every emergency. (White, *Patriarchs and Prophets*, p. 380)

The entire system of the revolving door of earthly powers is *wrath*. Wrath is what we get when God is sidelined. Its severity is coextensive to the degree that *we* have forsaken *Him*. Therefore, it is fallen humanity's unhappy situation to experience the reality that rejecting God results in being automatically punished with numerous curses as natural outcomes, not arbitrarily imposed by God. Among the effects of sin are included the "appointment" of leaders who have rejected God and who will rule from selfish principles. Such is an automatic reduction of freedom for the errant voter, acting as a built-in "punishment."

Even the necessity of parental guidance over children by a strong hand that curtails the "freedoms" of self-will is a result of sin. In other words, that we have to act "as God" over our children up to a certain age making their choices for them is not a model of God's perfect will. It is a necessary accommodation to the reality of living in a sin-cursed environment. We use inducements of rewards and threats of punishment to "guide" our children. (How to transition to and function within God's perfect will in childrearing is not easy, requiring careful and consistent consecration to God.) It is said that, when parents will not perform their duty to their children, "God Himself will take the case in hand. His restraining power will be in a measure removed from the agencies of evil, so that a train of circumstances will arise which will punish sin with sin" (White, *Patriarchs and Prophets*, p. 728). What this says, as pertaining to this discussion, is that when God takes the case into His own hands, He does not punish proactively but removes restraints on destructive forces and lets them wreak their effects on the self-willed.

"Permissive will" gives us earthly rulers who, on the one hand, can be a blessing and give us some measure of temporal security as well as the freedom to live according to our beliefs and preach the gospel; yet, on the other hand, even the best of governments take much from the people, as God warned the ancient Israelites. Not only will earthly governments forcefully require of us a portion of our earnings, but they will use it to engage in war. The people said, "…now make us a king to judge us like all the nations" (1 Sam. 8:5). God told them that a king would take everything from them by force, even their children, and they would "cry out in that day" because of the burdens they must bear under the yoke of earthly rulers; and He declared that He would not hear them—they would have to live with their choices (1 Sam. 8:18). God was against human rulers, in principle, but God Himself chose the first king, didn't He?

So, the kingdoms and ways of man are what they are. They have to govern in this world ravaged by the diseases brought on by sin—which manifests in various ways, on every street corner, in every home, and in every institution of man. Without human rules, Satanic principles would quickly decimate the earth and its inhabitants. However, it is not our function on this earth, as followers of Christ, to manage the governance and enforcements of Satan's systems. We must leave that business to God, Who has His angels in place to do that job and Who knows how and when He must, *being obliged* by the principles of righteousness—freedom, not force—stand down in His role as Protector and Sustainer.

Assyria as the Rod of God's Anger

How God uses evil nations to punish other evildoers is a conundrum to many. An uninformed reading of the biblical language makes it seem as though He arbitrarily puts in His oar to direct the affairs of men by the power of His might and they have no choice but to do His bidding, but it is not like this.

The "full cup" principle is when an entity reaches a point of losing its protection from God. Then other powers may come in, after His withdrawal of restraints. It seems as if God says, "I have been shown the door. I will honor that choice. I will leave and let the chips fall where they may." Notice how the Assyrian power was the weapon used of God against His professed people, a hypocritical people who had gone beyond the bounds of His protection.

> O Assyrian, the rod of mine anger, and the staff in their hand is mine indignation. I will send him against an hypocritical nation, and against the people of my wrath will I give him charge, to take the spoil, and to take the prey, and to tread them down like the mire of the streets. Howbeit he meaneth not so, neither doth his heart think so; but it is in his heart to destroy and cut off nations not a few. (Isaiah 10:5–7)

The *Seventh-day Adventist Bible Commentary* has some beneficial thoughts here:

> Assyria … had no idea that it was being used as a tool in the hands of the Lord. So far as Assyrian leaders were aware, their policies were determined entirely by their own selfish interests. In other words, **it was not the Spirit of the Lord that influenced Assyria to go against Israel and Judah, but the spirit of the evil one.** How, then, can it be said that Assyria was a tool in the hand of the Lord? God's protecting hand was withdrawn from the power against whom judgment had been decreed, and Assyria was permitted to work out her selfish, evil will. **It is thus that the Lord works out His sovereign will in a world that is in rebellion against Him. The purposes of men and demons are overruled to carry out the purposes of God.** (White, *The SDA Bible Commentary*, Vol. 4, pp. 151–152, emphasis added)

It is helpful to further clarify the ideas in that commentary, regarding the Lord *working out His sovereign will* and *overruling* in the affairs of men. On the surface, the language seems to say that He is yet involved in manipulation. It is not like this. God is not in the business of interfering with free will and moving pieces around on a gameboard to a predetermined outcome through the exercise of His superior knowledge, power, and skill. God knows the principles involved and that certain actions always bring certain results. He allows events to play out as they will, according to the perfect timing of His knowledge and judgment of the hearts of men, letting go of the winds of destruction as He departs from providing protective services. This is the working out of His sovereign will, but in a way that free choice can still be honored. This is His overruling, that the wicked be left without the interposition of mercy. It is language. He "overrules" by suspending protection, so that evil may have its way.

I'll keep pounding on this drum whenever I speak: *Evil punishes itself because it separates itself from the God of righteousness*, and therefore it can no longer enjoy the protective securities that come with right choice and remaining under the umbrella of God's beneficent power. Again, evil falls under the weight of its own burden when it exerts its will by force, for it subjects itself to the same, having forfeited the protection of a divine power. Self-determination accumulates up to the breaking point where God must judge—must make the call that He can no longer stay in the picture without forcing Himself there.

It is most interesting to note that the principles are unfailing and unerring. Cause is always followed by effect. Assyria was a "tool of God's anger," but He would not play favorites: Assyria's turn would come. That boastful, proud, and bloodthirsty nation would come to its own end:

> Wherefore it shall come to pass, that when the Lord hath performed his whole work upon mount Zion and on Jerusalem, I will punish the fruit of the stout heart of the king of Assyria, and the glory of his high looks. For he saith, By the strength of my hand I have done it, and by my wisdom; for I am prudent: and I have removed the bounds of the people, and have robbed their treasures, and I have put down the inhabitants like a valiant man: And my hand hath found as a nest the riches of the people: and as one gathereth eggs that are left, have I gathered all the earth; and there was none that moved the wing, or opened the mouth, or peeped. Shall the ax boast itself against him that heweth therewith? or shall the saw magnify itself against him that shaketh it? as if the rod should shake itself against them that lift it up, or as if the staff should lift up itself, as if it were no wood. Therefore shall the Lord, the Lord of hosts, send among his fat ones leanness; and under his glory he shall kindle a burning like the burning of a fire. (Isaiah 10:12–16)

As it was in ancient times, so it will be today. America's turn is coming. God's judgments are set to fall upon it and upon all nations, for their own wickedness. America and all the nations of the world today have their own "fat ones." Their boastful hearts will be punished, and under their glory will be a fire kindled.

CHAPTER 5

The True Spiritualism: A God of Force

> *"And the serpent said unto the woman, Ye shall not surely die: For God doth know that in the day ye eat thereof, then your eyes shall be opened, and ye shall be as gods, knowing good and evil."*
> Gen. 3:4–5

Some apologists for the standard view teach their listeners that the idea that God has not and *will not use divinely-directed force* to *proactively punish and destroy* rebels is *spiritualism* because they believe it is a misrepresentation of the Word of God. They will also level the charge that the "Character of God message" or "God does not kill" doctrine derives through *higher criticism* methods of handling the Word of God. We will talk about both of these ideas in this study, to see if they are so.

Spiritualism

The Spirit of Prophecy (SoP) talks about spiritualism in the following passages:

The warnings of the word of God regarding the perils surrounding the Christian church belong to us today. As in the days of the apostles men tried by tradition and philosophy to destroy faith in the Scriptures, so today, **by the pleasing sentiments of higher criticism, evolution, spiritualism, theosophy, and pantheism, the enemy of righteousness is seeking to lead souls into forbidden paths**. To many the Bible is as a lamp without oil, because they have turned their minds into channels of speculative belief that bring misunderstanding and confusion. **The work of higher criticism, in dissecting, conjecturing, reconstructing, is destroying faith in the Bible as a divine revelation**. It is robbing God's word of power to control, uplift, and inspire human lives. **By spiritualism, multitudes are taught to believe that desire is the highest law, that license is liberty, and that man is accountable only to himself.** The follower of Christ will meet with the 'enticing words' against which the apostle warned the Colossian believers. He will meet with **spiritualistic interpretations of the Scriptures**, but he is not to accept them. His voice is to be heard in clear affirmation of the eternal truths of the Scriptures. Keeping his eyes fixed on Christ, he is to move steadily forward in the path marked out, discarding all ideas that are not in harmony with His teaching. The truth of God is to be the subject for his contemplation and meditation. He is to regard the Bible as the voice of God speaking directly to him. Thus he will find the wisdom which is divine. **The knowledge of God as revealed in Christ is the knowledge that all who are saved must have. This is the knowledge that works transformation of character. Received into the life, it will re-create the soul in the image of Christ. This is the knowledge that God invites His children to receive, beside which all else is vanity and nothingness.** (White, *The Acts of the Apostles*, pp. 474–475, emphasis added)

We often think of spiritualism as seances, Ouija boards, and necromancy (conjuring/speaking with the departed). It includes those things, not as ends in themselves, but as Satan's media to convey his message and to evangelize the masses into his church of rebellion. At its very foundation it is the mantra of lawlessness: "Do as thou wilt, this is the whole of the law." It is based upon the claim of creature merit or innate goodness and that, to achieve righteousness in ourselves and revolutionize the world, we need only "follow our heart." The false doctrine of the immortality of the soul is not the only lie upon which Satan builds his deceptions. That doctrine falls into the category of *lies about created beings. Lies about God* are also part of the gamut of spiritualistic philosophies. Satan, as the author of confusion, wants to make sure we are deceived about identities. He confused angels about who they were, he confuses humans about who they are, and he would confuse every created being about who God is. In its broad sense, spiritualism is the voice of Satanic sophistries, all of which can be traced back and encapsulated in the fundamental lies told at the tree, for the purpose of inviting humanity to join him in his warfare against God.

The oppositional idea that *God will use His total command of any of the physical forces of creation to destroy rebels is the true spiritualism* and, if we read between the lines, we will find this serpentine insinuation at the tree of knowledge of good and evil. Interestingly, Satan weaves together lies about the creature with lies about God so that he may effectively convince humans that although they are supposedly immortal, God is guarding His own status as supreme by withholding the "realization" from them (about who they are) and that He will protect that status by the use of lethal force, if need be. That is saying a lot and I am perhaps getting ahead of myself. Let us unpack all of this.

When Satan denied that man would die for disobedience, saying to him and us, through his instructions to Eve, "You will absolutely *not* die! You will become an Ascended Master!," he was at the same time teaching that we could follow our own way—make up our own laws—and live in them. If we think about this clearly, we will find that he was saying that the threat of punishment and death would *not* be due to sin and it would certainly *not* be coming from him, for he was representing himself as a great benefactor of the race. He certainly would *not* be punishing us for rebelling against God, for disobeying God. There is only one logical conclusion. Satan was teaching that God would personally punish and kill the sinner or, as in the *Satanic* doctrines about hell fire (as opposed to the true biblical doctrine of hell fire), God would personally punish the sinner for choosing independence. The difference between standard annihilationism and eternal suffering is that one is finite and the other is not. Though these two are worlds apart in terms of cruelty, both are outright torture at the hands of God. In the standard (Satanic) concept of hellfire, the Divine is necessarily depicted as One who is actively using Divine power to sustain life and regenerate nerve and tissue for the purpose of inflicting unspeakable physical pain. Whether the fire burns for eternity or for a limited time, it would still be a voluntary imposition of and by God. Satan is satisfied if we believe either one of these lies about God.[3]

When we speak of the unquenchable fire of hell as a metaphorical device, the opposers will come in and accuse us of "spiritualizing away" their truth about hell, saying that we do not believe in a "literal" hell fire from God that burns up the flesh of the wicked while keeping them alive. To the defender of the standard view, "spiritualizing away" the Word of God means making a metaphor of the fire. While common sense tells us that God does not torture anybody, the Bible and the *Spirit of Prophecy* writings reveal the metaphor:

---

[3] The author has discussed in detail the nature of these fires in his book, *Awesome God: Songs of His Power, Volume 1*.

> Wherefore thus saith the LORD God of hosts, Because ye speak this word, behold, I will make **my words** in thy mouth **fire**, and this **people wood**, and **it shall devour them.** (Jeremiah 5:14, emphasis added)

> And say to the forest of the south, Hear the word of the LORD; Thus saith the Lord GOD; Behold, **I will kindle a fire in thee, and it shall devour** every green tree in thee, and every dry tree: the flaming flame **shall not be quenched**, and all faces from the south to the north **shall be burned therein**. And all flesh shall see that I the LORD have kindled it; **it shall not be quenched.** Then said I, Ah Lord GOD! they say of me, Doth he not speak parables? (Ezekiel 20:47–49, emphasis added)

Christ took the experience of this "fire" on His cross:

> Is it nothing to you, all ye that pass by? behold, and see if there be any sorrow like unto my **sorrow**, which is done unto me, wherewith the LORD hath afflicted me **in the day of his fierce anger. From above hath he sent a fire into my bones,** and it prevaileth against them: he hath spread a net for my feet, he hath turned me back: **he hath made me desolate** and faint all the day. (Lamentations 1:12, 13, emphasis added)

Ellen G. White defines the nature of this fire:

> We read of **chains of darkness** for the transgressor of God's law. We read of the **worm that dieth not**, and of the **fire that is not quenched**. Thus is **represented** the experience of every one who has permitted himself to be grafted into the stock of Satan, who has cherished sinful attributes. When it is too late, **he will see** that sin is the transgression of God's law. **He will realize** that because of transgression, his **soul is cut off from God**, and that God's wrath abides on him. **This is a fire unquenchable, and by**

it every unrepentant sinner will be destroyed. Satan strives constantly to lead men into sin, and he who is willing to be led, who refuses to forsake his sins, and despises forgiveness and grace, will suffer the result of his course. ("Christ and the Law," *Signs of the Times*, Apr. 14, 1898, par. 13, emphasis added)

Against every evildoer God's law utters **condemnation**. He may disregard that voice, he may seek to drown its warning, but in vain. It follows him. It makes itself heard. It destroys his peace. If unheeded, it pursues him to the grave. It bears witness against him at the judgment. **A quenchless fire, it consumes at last soul and body.** (White, *Education*, p. 144.5, emphasis added)

On "Spiritualizing Away" the Word of God

"Spiritualizing away" the word of God does not refer only to making metaphors of literal depictions but could also be defined by the reverse. For if inspiration declares a thing is a metaphor and defines the metaphor and yet we adamantly take hold of that metaphor and twist it into what we insist is a "literal" interpretation, we would actually be the ones who are "spiritualizing." For, in twisting the word of God, we are taking the Satanic part, promoting the lies that were told at the tree, all of which are "spiritualism." Spiritualism is not just classical occult activity, but all things that pertain to the lie that *sin* (which is separation from God through an agreement with lies) *does not of its own consequence bring death*.

Sin brings death, *not God*. If God were the One to bring death for defection from His government, then we have a tyranny after the order of human governance, which imposes punishment by arbitrary measure rather than by God's way which yields to the will of free moral agents, giving them up to the natural results of breaking laws that protect life and liberty. Satan says that death comes not from sin but from *God* punishing humans for sin. There is an irreconcilable difference between the two, with irreconcilable conclusions regarding the character of God and the nature of His government.

Again, the "unquenchable fire" is a metaphor for the psycho-emotional experience of the burden of sin.

> All are weighed down with burdens that only Christ can remove. The heaviest burden that we bear is the burden of sin. **If we were left to bear this burden, it would crush us**. But the Sinless One has taken our place. (White, *The Desire of Ages*, p. 328, emphasis added)

> It was **the burden of sin**, the sense of its terrible enormity, **of its separation of the soul from God**—it was this that broke the heart of the Son of God. (White, *Steps to Christ*, p. 13, emphasis added)

if it is separation from God that kills the finally impenitent—and yet we believe that God is the One Who kills the sinner—then we are saying that it is God Who causes the separation. But God does not cause the separation.

The "burden of sin" causes this "separation of the soul from God." It is the realization of which Ellen White says brings the death of the wicked in the end—the sinner "**will realize** that because of transgression, his soul is cut off from God, and that **God's wrath** (see Deut. 31:16–18) abides on him. **This** is a fire unquenchable, and **by it** every unrepentant sinner will be destroyed" ("Christ and the Law," *Signs of the Times*, Apr. 14, 1898, par. 13, emphasis added). The guilt of transgression follows the sinner right on through to the second death and unremedied it will "consume," at last, both "soul and body" (see White, *Education*, p. 144).

Therefore, if it is separation from God that kills the finally impenitent—and yet we believe that God is the One Who kills the sinner—then we are saying that it is God Who causes the separation. But God does not cause the separation. The separation is the choice of the free moral agent.

"God never forsakes people or individuals until they forsake Him" (White, *Selected Messages*, Book 2, p. 378).

God does not separate us from Himself. *We do that ourselves*. And in keeping with the principles of freedom, God must allow us to do it. This means He must, at last, turn off the current of life that flows from Himself to the impenitent, for this will be their informed choice at last. "And death shall be chosen rather than life by all of the residue of them that remain" (Jer. 8:3).

There is no "new power"—i.e., a physical power wrought into effect by the hand of God—that comes in to dispose of the wicked. They instead bring into play a chain of events whereby the power of God is taken away. For His power is only to uphold and protect. Therefore, *the showing of God's power is to see the effect of its absence*! Notice that against Pharaoh and his Egypt, no power of this kind was employed by God. *No "new" power*!

> Pharaoh had his sowing time, and he also had his reaping time. He sowed resistance and obstinacy. He sowed the seed in the soil. **No new power was put into operation by God**. The seed was left to spring up; the man was permitted to act out his true character. When the Lord sees unbelief in the heart against light and evidence, **all he has to do is to let the human agent alone**; for the seed put into the soil will bring forth seed after its kind …. The character revealed by Pharaoh is similar to that of all the impenitent. **God destroys no man; but after a time the wicked are given up to the destruction they have wrought for themselves.** ("Words to the Young," *The Youth's Instructor*, Nov. 30, 1893, par. 6, emphasis added)

It is not spiritualism to teach that the wages of sin is death. *It is spiritualism to say that God pays those wages*, by personally torturing and killing the sinner for rejecting Him. To take the key statements of the Bible and the Spirit of Prophecy that define the manner of the death of the wicked and insist that they come into line with the human version of justice and punishment is the true spiritualism.

William Tyndale on Bible Symbolism

Note the words of William Tyndale (1494–1539), who was the first person to translate the Bible into English from its original Greek and Hebrew and was the first to print the Bible in English ("Tyndale Bible," Wikipedia, https://1ref.us/stra5 [accessed Nov. 30, 2022]). This is what he believed, what I believe, and what is attested to by Ellen White who wrote, "The language of the Bible should be explained according to its obvious meaning, unless a symbol or figure is employed" (White, *The Great Controversy*, p. 598).

The "worm that dieth not" and the "fire that is not quenched" are synonymous biblical figures, used in the previously quoted Spirit of Prophecy passage ("Christ and the Law," *Signs of the Times*, Apr. 14, 1898, par. 13). They are *symbols*, they are not physical worms and physical fires. They are *representations* of the burden of sin and its destructive effects.

William Tyndale penned the following:

Thou shalt understand therefore that the scripture hath but one sense which is the literal sense. And that literal sense is the root and ground of all, and the anchor that never faileth whereunto if thou cleave thou canst never err or go out of the way (Tyndale, *Doctrinal Treatises and Introduction to Different Portions of the Holy Scriptures*, p. 283).

Neverthelater, the scripture useth proverbs, similitudes, riddles or allegories as all other speeches do, but that which the proverb, similitude, riddle or allegory signifieth is ever the literal sense which thou must seek out diligently (Tyndale, *The Obedience of a Christian Man*, p. 156).

What I have brought for your consideration is not to be taken lightly. These are deep things, and they require an application of mental power. We do well not to read these things quickly nor brush them carelessly aside. They are for us to study intently that we may understand their full implications. If one cannot take the time to examine the matter with earnest intent, then it is best to not get involved in the conversation, for there must be a willingness to "seek out diligently" what is the literal sense of the figures employed in the biblical language of wrath.

The Bible student has an obligation in matters of challenges to long-held traditional beliefs, whether in the role of making a challenge or receiving one:

> **The Bible must not be interpreted to suit** the ideas of men, however long they may have held these ideas to be true. We are not to accept the opinion of commentators as the voice of God; they were erring mortals like ourselves. God has given reasoning powers to us as well as to them. We should **make the Bible its own expositor.** (White, *Gospel Workers*, p. 126, emphasis added)

> All should be careful about presenting new views of Scripture before they have given these points thorough study, and are fully prepared to sustain them from the Bible. **Introduce nothing that will cause dissension, without clear evidence that in it God is giving a special message for this time.** (White, *Gospel Workers*, p. 126, emphasis added)

> At no period of time has man learned all that can be learned of the word of God. **There are yet new views of truth to be seen, and much to be understood of the character and attributes of God** …. This is a most valuable study, taxing the intellect, and giving strength to the mental ability. After diligently searching the word, **hidden treasures are discovered, and the lover of truth breaks out in triumph**. (White, *Fundamentals of Christian Education*, p. 444, emphasis added)

Why does the student break out in triumph? Why are these views, to the Seventh-day Adventist, considered as *"new"* views? These are important questions for, if the new view was that God destroys the wicked by the power of force, it would not be a new view. This was the standard view when she penned these words and remains to this day as the Adventist position. The triumph is in realizing that God's character is such that it does not allow Him to ever use force or bring pain to people, even the vilest of haters. He allows them to experience pain, but this is not the same as Him causing it. It will break His heart to see their final end transpire. He is not the One to bring it about by power, but by revelation.

This is *the* study that divides the sheep from the goats in the finalizing of the great controversy. This is a big claim, I know, yet it is true:

> Yet Satan was not then destroyed. The angels did not even then understand all that was involved in the great controversy. The principles at stake were to be more fully revealed. And for the sake of man, Satan's existence must be continued. Man as well as angels must see the contrast between the Prince of light and the prince of darkness. He must choose whom he will serve. (White, *The Desire of Ages*, p. 761)

> Jesus Christ is the Restorer. The apostate, Satan, is the destroyer. **Here is the conflict** between the Prince of life and the prince of this world, the power of darkness. (White, Letter 34, 1896, emphasis added)

> By the same misrepresentation of the character of God as he had practiced in heaven, causing Him to be regarded as severe and tyrannical, Satan induced man to sin. And having succeeded thus far, he declared that God's unjust restrictions had led to man's fall, as they had led to his own rebellion. (White, *The Great Controversy*, p. 500)

[Note: The exposition of God's character and methods as they truly are will undo the rebellion for any who desire to be in harmony with God. Those who have sold themselves to the god of this world, however, will cling to the system of rewards and punishments that values raw power for self-benefit above all else.]

It is Satan's constant effort to misrepresent the character of God, the nature of sin, and the real issues at stake in the great controversy. His sophistry lessens the obligation of the divine law and gives men license to sin. At the same time **he causes them to cherish false conceptions of God** so that they regard Him with fear and hate rather than with love. The cruelty inherent in his own character is attributed to the Creator; it is embodied in systems of religion and expressed in modes of worship. Thus the minds of men are blinded, and Satan secures them as his agents to war against God. By perverted conceptions of the divine attributes, heathen nations were led to believe human sacrifices necessary to secure the favor of Deity; and horrible cruelties have been perpetrated under the various forms of idolatry. (White, *The Great Controversy*, p. 569, emphasis added)

Now therefore write ye this song for you, and teach it the children of Israel: put it in their mouths, that this song may be a witness for me against the children of Israel. (Deuteronomy 31:19)

The God of Force; Controversy with the Gods of Egypt and the Results of Freedom

Let us make some comments on the biblical account of the exodus in the context of the great controversy, which is how we should always examine Bible stories. We have been taught of a thundering God of Force, the "Awesome God" of the popular evangelical praise song, with lightning in His fists, in Whom we had "better believe." He is a God of force, yet the big question is this, "Did He march through Egypt wielding His power as a sword, or did He take His power away from Egypt and bless His people with it as He marshalled them away from that dark land?" In delivering the Israelites, God pushed the waters apart by applying His creative power to save, which is always how He exerts power. When His purpose was accomplished, as a freedom-loving and freedom-giving God,

He would no longer have a right to exert power to save and keep the Egyptians because they had rejected Him and chosen other gods. This was a showdown of Pharaoh's doing. Pharaoh had issued the challenge, "Who is God...?" (see Exod. 5:2). The Egyptians relied upon their own gods to provide protection. For God to disallow the demonstration would make him a God of force (compulsion), protecting them against their will. Further, they would only continue to deny Him while attributing any blessings and protections to their gods which were no-gods. So it is that the Lord proclaimed, "Against all the gods of Egypt I will execute judgment" (Exod. 12:12). God was obligated to allow Satan to have his prey, because in choosing other gods they were choosing Satan, for behind those gods, there was the power of the enemy to trick the Egyptians. Therefore, there was a showdown of power in Pharoah's headquarters and in the land of Egypt. Satan, through Pharaoh and his court, had issued a challenge to the directive of the Almighty to let His people go. "I will not let them go" he countered (see Exod. 5:2). Therefore, the I AM, in strict justice, had to let those gods [Satan] do as they [he] would, with the result that those who had chosen those gods would be subject to them. Would Satan bless them or destroy them? He is given leeway to act in either direction. "Satan has control of all whom God does not especially guard. He will favor and prosper some in order to further his own designs, and he will bring trouble upon others and lead men to believe that it is God who is afflicting them" (White, *The Great Controversy*, p. 589).

If Satan had been able at that time and under those circumstances to keep up the winds that God created to make a way of escape for His people, he may have done it. However, it probably would not have been the better of his options. Satan would have inspired the Egyptians to credit their gods for doing it, of course, and God's people would have been destroyed besides. However, I believe that even if Satan *could have* worked in this manner, he saw a better opportunity to immediately accomplish the three major objectives that constitute the sum of his warfare against God—his "constant effort to misrepresent" three things:

1. The character of God. (Is He a God of love and freedom or a God of arbitrary force?)
2. The nature of sin. (Will sin result in destruction without help from God?)
3. The real issues at stake in the great controversy. (*Who* is the Creator, Sustainer, and Healer, and *who* is the destroyer? See Letter 34, 1896, cited earlier.)

God was under no obligation to keep the Egyptians alive and, in fact was not able to save the Egyptians. It was against their will. So he left them to Satan and Satan either *chose* not to keep the waters or he *could* not keep the waters. I believe he could not keep them but, even if he could, he would not, because he would do better to use this situation through all time to keep up the lie that God is a destroyer by proactive force. He has been very successful in doing this, and it is why we are even having this discussion among professed Christians. Another reason that Satan would not move to preserve his own is because he loves any mass destruction of the wicked, for in it he can take thousands to a Christless grave and save himself from suffering for their sins, as depicted in the scapegoat scenario of the Day of Atonement celebration proceedings. "Storm and tempest, war and bloodshed,—in these things he delights, and thus he gathers in his harvest" ("A Time of Trouble," *Review and Herald*, Sept. 17, 1901, par. 9).

> *Another reason that Satan would not move to preserve his own is because he loves any mass destruction of the wicked, for in it he can take thousands to a Christless grave*

> Also it would be for his own interest to keep from Jesus as many as possible. For the sins of those who are redeemed by the blood of Christ will at last be rolled back upon the originator of sin, and he must bear their punishment, while those who do not

accept salvation through Jesus will suffer the penalty of their own sins. (White, *Early Writings*, p. 178)

Higher Criticism and the Bible Language

In our opening quote from the pen of inspiration we find the mention of "higher criticism" being brought to bear upon the Bible so that doubt may be cast upon it as a reliable guide to faith and practice. Proponents of the message of God's character find themselves scrutinized as higher critics. What is nothing less than the due diligence of proper exegesis is subjected to pejorative relabeling by critics of the message as "higher criticism." Labeling things with broad strokes is not productive of actual progress in a discussion. Labeling tends toward closing a discussion. It is attempting to steer minds away from examining what is being said.

It is not a faulty hermeneutic principle to use the text to interpret the text. As in our example given earlier, when the "fire unquenchable" is defined by inspiration as cognizant realization of the truth about the burden of sin and its results on the human psyche, we believe it and we apply it to our reading and understanding of the Bible. When wrath is defined in Scripture as Divine departure (the "hiding of His face"), we apply the meaning given by the prophets, for indeed the prophets are subject to the prophets. A man's speculative meanings are worthless, leading away from the light contained within the writings. This is a serious matter, for error is calculated by the enemy to secure the mind and soul into "everlasting chains of darkness" (2 Peter 2:4; Jude 6).

What is also not understood is that there are elements in the schools of "criticism" that are highly disparaged by mainstream Christian fundamentalism. Unlike the mainstream, Seventh-day Adventist theology has typology at its very core. Without typology, particularly that of the typical sanctuary economy, Adventism falls as a theological system. Typology comes under the roof of the historical-grammatical method which is in the house of "higher criticism." Thus we find it to be a broad label and not useful in this discussion, except to its enemies, who find it a convenient dragnet in which they think to catch their opponents as bad fish to be tossed back into the sea of heresy. Ellen White was in many cases a "higher critic" while writing under inspiration. Anytime we go into the text, into history, into the culture, we are employing critical methods. To not do so places one in the camp of literalism that admonishes us to "take the Bible just as it reads."[4] The product tends to the boorish and clumsy side and winds up presenting a Bible that appears to be full of contradictions, making it appear goofy or nonsensical. This is the fuel that bakes the bread of atheism, subjecting the Bible and the God of the Bible to scorn and ridicule.

How are we to understand the Bible language? When it says He will destroy, what principle of operation brings about such a thing? "The Lord will do **just what He has declared that he would**—He will **withdraw His blessings** from the earth and **remove His protecting care** from those who are rebelling against His law and teaching and forcing others to do the same. **Satan has control of all whom God does not especially guard**. He will favor and prosper some, in order to further his own designs, and he will bring trouble upon others and lead men to believe that it is God who is afflicting them" (White, *The Great Controversy*, p. 589, emphasis added). There is no way to prove that God has another way of "bringing" destruction other than by removing restraints, *removing His power*. To insist that He has a second modality of destruction through *the exertion of power* is not viable. There is absolutely no Bible or Spirit of Prophecy-derived hermeneutic principle that would support this. Further, it is not found in Christ, who is our primary example and touchstone for interpreting what is truly happening in any given narrative of the apparent Divine use of violence or force to put down rebellion. This carnal modality derives from the human desire for vengeance and from a surface reading of the Bible. It is made possible by ignoring this Hebrew maxim:

---

[4] "Taking the Bible just as it reads" does not mean literalism (obtaining meaning by applying the modern usages and definitions of a foreign culture, mindset, tradition, language, and etymology, while ignoring the historical, cultural, and literary context). "Taking the Bible just as it reads" rather means to *believe the metanarrative of Scripture—i.e., the gospel story of the fall and redemption.*

"It was a maxim among the Jews that a failure to do good, when one had opportunity, was to do evil; to neglect to save life was to kill" (White, *The Desire of Ages*, p. 286). "God destroys no man" is the plain teaching of the word of God. Yet we can simultaneously say that God destroys. He does this *not* in the sense of a personal application of His power. God destroys man only in the sense of the Hebrew maxim, which is the "looking the other way," "hiding of His face," or "giving up" the person or group to the results of bad choices. Our critics will attempt to derail minds on this by falsely calling out the application of the Hebrew modality of thought and expression as "higher criticism." Apparently, there is a nefarious principle in operation here, wherein the originator of a thought or a mode of expression must be subjected to whatever construct somebody else may impose upon the language used, especially when that original communicator—due to silencing or death—has no say in what is meant by their words.

The spiritualism inherent in the teaching that God uses violence to win the great controversy is from Satan, the serpent in the tree, that destroyer, who claimed that sin will not destroy us, inferring that God will do it by force, for supposedly this is what His character and government are about. Satan's masterful attribution of His own character to God has been the basis of the great controversy from the outset, and we are now involved in this core issue. The end of the controversy comes when God's character is at last revealed fully. Part of this process of revelation must incorporate the study of how to read the Bible language. Satan has been able to take full advantage of the idiomatic language in his desire to keep minds locked into this dark paradigm of belief in a God Who has two ways to destroy—one by removing power and giving over and the other by pulling rank of superior power and applying force to end any further rebellious choice. However, if God can use force to achieve His ends, what further need is there for anything else? What is it that He would be trying to demonstrate? We cannot force anyone to see how good and loving we are. For if God would apply force to move things along toward a victory for His kingdom and to finally end the rebellion, then He may as well just have declared this to be a *"My way or the highway dictatorship"* from the very outset and dispensed with the charade. Everyone knows God has superior power, as He is the Creator. This is not where the dispute lies. The conflict is between principles of freedom of choice and force. One power obtains only that which comes through a creative and sustaining endeavor in an environment of freedom of choice, while the other metes out punishment and destruction for non-compliance with authority. Love has nothing to do with it. "Jesus Christ is the Restorer. Satan, the apostate, is the destroyer. **Here** is the conflict between the Prince of life and the prince of this world, the power of darkness" (White, *Christ Triumphant*, p. 247, emphasis added).

That is a nail in a sure place. Satan uses overwhelming power to destroy his enemies. God does not. He appeals to reason and to demonstration. Until we get this right, the controversy is not over.

> By the same misrepresentation of the character of God as he had practiced in heaven, causing Him to be regarded as severe and tyrannical, Satan induced man to sin. And having succeeded thus far, he declared that God's unjust restrictions had led to man's fall, as they had led to his own rebellion. (White, *The Great Controversy*, p. 500)

Satan Hides Behind Bible Language

> Their sufferings are often **represented as** a punishment visited upon them by the direct decree of God. It is thus that the **great deceiver** seeks to **conceal** his own work. By stubborn rejection of divine love and mercy, the Jews had caused the **protection** of God to be **withdrawn** from them, and Satan was **permitted** to rule them according to his will. The horrible cruelties enacted in the destruction of Jerusalem are a demonstration of Satan's vindictive power over those who yield to his control. (White, *The Great Controversy*, p. 35, emphasis added)

Note that the Jews' sufferings are "represented as punishment by decree and some go further to even suggest that God controls evil forces to make them do His bidding. Where might we find these representations? The Bible! Yes! Although this is *the language* of the Bible, it is not *the teaching* of the Bible. It is rather a misreading of the Bible. Satan is there parked on the shoulders of men, whispering in their ears that this is how God does things. It is not hard to understand why the lie is so successful because—from the standpoint of carnal affinity with the lies of Satan, from the experience of this world that operates on the judicial paradigm of exemplary deterrence which is effected by retributive penalization (lex talionis—the "law of retaliation," which is eye-for-eye justice)—it is an easy thing for men to disregard the Hebrew idiom and see a God who is like them. They see that God is *righteous* and He is *almighty* and He apparently uses His omnipotence to do what needs to be done to establish His good purposes. Thus, the principle of "might is right" is embedded like a virus into our operating system. This idea makes its way out of religious circles and into the general world, portraying a dark picture of a God who has moved in history to horribly punish an entire race of people for the sins of their fathers in crucifying Christ. Hitler made good capital of this, rounding up those "Christ killers" as worthy of death.

The Power of *Sin* Is Death

"The sting of death is sin; and the strength of sin is the law" (1 Cor. 15:56). The law is the protocol upon which life is established and the only way in which it may be sustained. It is an intrinsic law. It was not a new thing, some arbitrary fabrication. It is the eternal law of the eternal God, brought down to suit the needs of His new creation of the human race for the assurance of its continued enjoyment of life in a perfect universe. "For the commandment is a lamp; and the law is light; and reproofs of instruction are the way of life" (Prov. 6:23). "In him was life; and the life was the light of men" (John 1:4). "The Creator of man ... proclaimed **the eternal**

law" ("God's Desire for His People," *Review and Herald*, Aug. 26, 1909, par. 9, emphasis added).

> They can say, I believe on Christ that He is my Saviour, but why do they disregard His law which is the **transcript of His character**? When they disregard the law of Jehovah they disregard the Lord Jesus Christ. (1888 Manuscript, p. 128, emphasis added)

> Jesus Christ the same yesterday, and to day, and for ever. (Hebrews 13:8)

Sin will pay its wages. This is its strength: it brings death. No new power is required.

> Pharaoh had ... his reaping time. **No new power** [arbitrary power applied by Deity as discretionary, volitional power] was put into operation by God .... When the Lord sees unbelief in the heart against light and evidence, **all He has to do is let the human agent alone** .... **God destroys no man**; but after a time **the wicked are given up** to the destruction they have wrought for themselves. ("Words to the Young," *The Youth's Instructor*, Nov. 30, 1893, par. 6, emphasis added)

This principle of "letting alone" applies to *all* the wicked, not just to Pharoah. The destruction wrought out by sin comes upon all who reject God, and this is the power that works their end. God does not employ new power, or power newly brought to bear, upon them in order to kill them. God does not "do" it in the ordinary modern sense that we understand "doing." He only "does it" in the Hebraic idiomatic sense of *allowing* it to occur, while we hasten to add that He *allows* it—not out of any arbitrary and imaginary mark of impatience on His part—but only when the issues are clear in the minds of every living, free moral agent in the universe. Then He is going to allow the impenitent to have their suicide and everyone will understand that it is suicide. "O that they were wise, that they understood this, that they would consider their latter end!" (Deuteronomy 32:29). "The anger of the LORD shall not return, until he have executed, and till he have performed the thoughts of his heart: in the latter days ye shall consider it perfectly" (Jeremiah 23:20).

Jeremiah says it twice:

"Behold, the whirlwind of the LORD goeth forth with fury, a continuing whirlwind: it shall fall with pain upon the head of the wicked. The fierce anger of the LORD shall not return, until he have done it, and until he have performed the intents of his heart: in the latter days ye shall consider it" (Jer. 30:23, 24). The apologist for the "consistent view" of the Bible language and God's character is not afraid to freely take up discussion of all the quotations, both the ones that say God destroys and the ones that make it clear *how* He destroys, and to bring them into harmony.

Divine Wrath Is Not Arbitrary

> He [Satan] declared that its [the law's] precepts could not be obeyed and that the penalties of transgression were bestowed arbitrarily.[5] (White, *Prophets and Kings*, p. 311)

---

[5] *Arbitrary*—in this application does not denote "RANDOMNESS" or "CAPRICIOUSNESS," for believers will largely agree that God is not like that; rather, the sense of the word to which we should appeal when it is said that "nothing God does is arbitrary" is in contrast to the more common usage. The proper denotation of the word *arbitrary* as it applies to our discussion is "DISCRETIONARY," or "VOLITIONAL." God doesn't just decide He's had enough and choose to give over at a point that is determined by nothing but Himself. Nor does He discretely make a choice as to where He is going to draw that line in the sand, as if to say, "cross it and you're finished." The only discretion that comes into this picture is that, in His judgment, He determines what our choices are and how fixed they are and–by virtue of the fact that He knows our mind and heart—He gives us over to those choices. His objectivity is perfect, as it is based upon the wisdom of an omniscient love. Further, God does not ever volunteer His wrath. We call it up by our choices. When our choices are for self and Satan's ways, we are giving ourselves over to the enemy and rejecting God. Satan knows it, and God knows it. According to the terms of the great controversy, which are that God must demonstrate the superiority of His character and government of love over and against Satan's system of self-exaltation which will use force and deceit, God must honor Satan's claims to the subjects of his kingdom when their hearts are hardened against the principles of life, against *Him*. Divine wrath is not volitional on His part, it is *acquired* by the human agent.]

The True Spiritualism: A God of Force   69

The use of punishing force or capital punishment against beings struck with a terminal disease is an arbitrary execution. We simply must not go there in our reading of the Bible or the Spirit of Prophecy. Here are some well-known passages by Ellen White that those who support the traditional view will set forth as "proof" that God will choose to exercise physical power to punish sin:

> God will vindicate His law and deliver His people. Satan and all who have joined him in rebellion will be cut off. Sin and sinners will perish, root and branch, (Malachi 4:1),—Satan the root, and his followers the branches. The word will be fulfilled to the prince of evil, "Because thou hast set thine heart as the heart of God … I will destroy thee, O covering cherub, from the midst of the stones of fire …. Thou shalt be a terror, and never shalt thou be any more." Then "the wicked shall not be: yea, thou shalt diligently consider his place, and it shall not be;" "they shall be as though they had not been" Ezekiel 28:6–19; Psalm 37:10; Obadiah 16. (White, *The Desire of Ages*, p. 763)

Yet, to our amazement, they glide right on over the next paragraph which sheds light such as would forbid them from interpreting it the way they do:

> **This is not an act of arbitrary power on the part of God**. The rejecters of His mercy reap that which they have sown. **God is the fountain of life; and when one chooses the service of sin, he separates from God, and thus cuts himself off from life**. He is 'alienated from the life of God.' Christ says, 'All they that hate Me love death.' Ephesians 4:18; Proverbs 8:36. God gives them existence for a time that they may develop their character and reveal their principles. This accomplished, they receive **the results of their own choice.**[6] By a life of rebellion, Satan and all

---

[6] Those results are *cause and effect principles of sin*, which are that sin has the inherent seeds of death and will destroy the sinner; we dare not say that *sin causes God to kill you*, for this is Satan's line.

who unite with him place themselves so out of harmony with God that His very presence is to them a consuming fire. The glory of Him who is love will destroy them. (White, *The Desire of Ages*, 764, emphasis added)

The Sword of Truth a Cleaver that Hastens on the Day of the Lord

As the message goes forth in the loud cry, they will crucify Christ again in His people, who have come to more fully understand, appreciate, and exemplify His character. What is occurring now, in the hearts of those living their lives on the broad road, is a resistance and hardening in response to the revelation of God. As we relate the truth about God, it is a tremendous thing to consider that we are handling a double-edged sword and, while doing the work of bringing believers to fully appreciate the glory of God, we are hardening hearts of others. This is the sword that Christ said He was bringing to the earth.

> *God is the fountain of life; and when one chooses the service of sin, he separates from God, and thus cuts himself off from life.*

> Whosoever therefore shall confess me before men, him will I confess also before my Father which is in heaven. But whosoever shall deny me before men, him will I also deny before my Father which is in heaven. Think not that I am come to send peace on earth: I came not to send peace, but a sword. For I am come to set a man at variance against his father, and the daughter against her mother, and the daughter in law against her mother in law. and a man's foes [shall be] they of his own household.[7] (Matthew 10:32–36)

---

[7] Including the household of faith.

By telling the truth about God, we are destroying sinners, either by drawing them to God and His ways for healing or, through the rejection of the message, driving them to their eternal ruin.

> The light that shines upon our path, the truth that commends itself to our consciences, will condemn and destroy the soul, or sanctify and transform it. (White, *Testimonies for the Church*, Vol. 1, p. 307)

> Let ministers and people remember that **gospel truth ruins if it does not save**. The soul that refuses to listen to the invitations of mercy from day to day can soon listen to the most urgent appeals without an emotion stirring his soul. (White, *Testimonies for the Church*, Vol. 5, 134, emphasis added)

Our gospel message is simple: choose ye this day whom ye will serve. Jesus saves souls by creating in them His living righteousness. Satan and sin destroy souls by holding them captive to the lies about God, making them like himself, as fuel for the fire of separation from God, subjecting them to the same chains of everlasting darkness that are irrevocably fastened upon his own heart. Any confusion on this matter is brought about by eating the fruit from the tree of spiritualism.

CHAPTER 6

The Angel, the Sword, and the Tree

*"All that the Father giveth me shall come to me;
and him that cometh to me I will in no wise cast out."*
John 6:37

*"Blessed are they which do hunger and thirst after righteousness:
for they shall be filled."*
Matt. 5:6

"For my flesh is meat indeed, and my blood is drink indeed."
John 6:55

Part I: An online three-way study with Elder Demetrius Leach,[8] May 12–14, 2017

[The following is adapted from a social media discussion, edited for clarity.]

---

[8] Independent Seventh-day Adventist minister and apostle of Christ.

Jennifer: In Genesis Chapter 3, it says the angels have flaming swords. If God doesn't use force and violence, why would the angels need swords? I don't believe God uses violence or force but some people bring this text up. What's the answer for this?

Demetrius: "So he drove out the man; and he placed at the east of the garden of Eden Cherubims, and a flaming sword which turned every way, to keep the way of the tree of life" (Gen. 3:24). Jennifer, it is usual that we assume the Bible to be saying what it is not. You mentioned that in Genesis 3 it says the angels have flaming swords. If you check the Scripture carefully you will realize that it says "Cherubims, *and* a flaming sword." We assume that the flaming sword was in the hand of the angels. The Scripture does not say that. The Scripture says that there were two things present, angels AND a flaming sword. We then need to allow Scripture to interpret what is meant. [Note: Inspiration declares the sword was not actual but a visual representation.]

Strong angels, **with beams of light representing flaming swords** turning in every direction, were placed as sentinels to guard the way of the tree of life from the approach of Satan and the guilty pair. ("Redemption– No. 1," *Review and Herald*, February 24, 1874, par. 20, emphasis added)

Jennifer: Okay, it doesn't specifically say the angels are holding a flaming sword. That is assumed. In the Bible, the sword is God's word when He speaks. Revelation 2:16 says, "Repent; or else I will come unto thee quickly, and will fight against them with the sword of my mouth."

Demetrius: Correct. A careful examination of the Scripture will explain what is meant. Let's go through a progression of thought. Our first thought is that those angels were placed there to be against man. However, consider this text of Scripture.

> But to which of the angels said he at any time, Sit on my right hand, until I make thine enemies thy footstool? Are they not all ministering spirits, sent forth to minister for them who shall be heirs of salvation? (Hebrews 1:13, 14)

Note that they are called *ministering spirits*. They are sent to minister to man. Hence, those angels placed at the garden were to minister to Adam's need. We also see this illustrated in Jacob's case. "And he dreamed, and behold a ladder set up on the earth, and the top of it reached to heaven: and behold the angels of God ascending and descending on it" (Gen. 28:12).

It is very interesting that Jesus referred to this when speaking with Nathaniel: "And he saith unto him, Verily, verily, I say unto you, Hereafter ye shall see heaven open, and the angels of God ascending and descending upon the Son of man" (John 1:51).

Therefore, Jesus is the ladder. The angels were ascending and descending upon the ladder which is Christ. This means that the angels were communicating to man the mysteries of redemption. Hence, those angels at the garden were there to communicate with man the mysteries of redeeming love. Since they were ascending and descending upon the Son of Man, then they were communicating Christ to man. But what is Jesus called? "And the Word was made flesh, and dwelt among us, (and we beheld his glory, the glory as of the only begotten of the Father,) full of grace and truth" (John 1:14).

Jesus is called *the word of God*. Therefore, these angels were communicating the word of God to man. As you rightly said, the word of God is the sword. Here are two references.

> For the word of God is quick, and powerful, and sharper than any twoedged sword, piercing even to the dividing asunder of soul and spirit, and of the joints and marrow, and is a discerner of the thoughts and intents of the heart. (Hebrews 4:12)

And take the helmet of salvation, and the sword of the Spirit, which is the word of God. (Ephesians 6:17)

Now, Jesus is also seen with a sword. But where is this sword? "And he had in his right hand seven stars: and out of his mouth went a sharp twoedged sword: and his countenance was as the sun shineth in his strength" (Rev. 1:16).

The sword is coming out of His mouth. It is not in his hand. Again, notice what He says about that which comes from the mouth. "O generation of vipers, how can ye, being evil, speak good things? for out of the abundance of the heart the mouth speaketh" (Matt. 12:34).

What was stored in the heart of Jesus? "Thy word have I hid in mine heart, that I might not sin against thee" (Psalm 119:11). The word of God was stored in the heart of Christ. It is the word, then, that comes from His mouth. But this word that comes from His mouth is life-giving. "It is the spirit that quickeneth; the flesh profiteth nothing: the words that I speak unto you, they are spirit, and they are life" (John 6:63).

Christ's word is life. If we turn from the Word, death is the only result. Jesus Himself said that it is the word that will condemn. "He that rejecteth me, and receiveth not my words, hath one that judgeth him: the word that I have spoken, the same shall judge him in the last day" (John 12:48). For this reason, Jesus said that unless we repent, He will fight against us. "Repent; or else I will come unto thee quickly, and will fight against them with the sword of my mouth" (Rev. 2:16).

Jennifer: So the angels came to encourage, and the flaming sword represents God's Word that they were not cut off completely?

Demetrius: Correct. Those angels at the garden possessed the Word of life, But it seemed as though they were preventing us from accessing the tree of life. But let's look a little closer at the text. "… to keep the way of the tree of life." To keep the way means to preserve the way so that it would not be lost to man forever.

Genesis 3:24, then, is one of the most encouraging texts in the Bible. It shows the plan of salvation, the heart of God, and the ministry of the angels working on behalf of fallen men. God was not trying to protect the tree; He was seeking to save man. Salvation was not in eating of the physical tree but in being reconnected to the spiritual tree of life, Christ Himself.

Jennifer: Well, it says the sword turned every way to keep the way of the tree of life. The definition of *way* in the Hebrew (H1870) "derek" (deh'-rek) is as follows: way, road, distance, journey, manner, path, journey, direction, manner, habit, of course of life (figuratively), of moral character (figuratively).

Demetrius: It must turn every way. Whatever way we choose we must find a crucified Savior in our path. We can never press on in sin unless we trample upon a crucified Savior. "Jesus saith unto him, 'I am the way, the truth, and the life: no man cometh unto the Father, but by me'" (John 14:6).

Jennifer: *Keep* is defined in the Hebrew, H8104, as "shamar" (shaw-mar'), to keep, guard, observe, give heed; (Qal) to keep, have charge of, to keep, guard, keep watch and ward, protect, save life, watch, watchman (participle), to watch for, wait for, to watch, observe, to keep, retain, treasure up (in memory), to keep (within bounds), restrain, to observe, celebrate, keep (sabbath or covenant or commands), perform (vow), to keep, preserve, protect, to keep, reserve; (Niphal) to be on one's guard, take heed, take care, beware, to keep oneself, refrain, abstain, to be kept, be guarded; (Piel) to keep, pay heed; (Hithpael) to keep oneself from.

Demetrius: Jesus is the way. The angels keep the way. They preserve and protect that way, that it would not be lost to man. It is not against man at all. "Thy way, O God, is in the sanctuary: who is so great a God as our God?" (Ps. 77:13).

God's way is in the sanctuary. Hence, the angels were guarding the way to the sanctuary. The sanctuary is a temple. But note again: "And I saw no temple therein: for the Lord God Almighty and the Lamb are the temple of it" (Rev. 21:22).

Christ is the way and God is the temple. The angels were preserving the path back to God through Jesus Christ. This is simply the way God teaches, and we can only understand what He is saying by rightly dividing the word of truth, by comparing Scripture with Scripture. We allow the Bible to interpret itself.

> Jennifer: This is the same idea that A. T. Jones presents about the designated roads always kept in repair, making it very easy for man to find refuge in the city if he made a mistake and accidentally killed someone. Also, in the book of Jeremiah, God talks about His willingness to forgive and heal backsliding over and over.
>
> Demetrius: That is the nature of God, from Genesis to Revelation. Unless we find *this* in the scripture, we are wasting time.
>
> Jennifer: These things are such food for the soul, and you can't help but love God.
>
> Kevin: Demetrius, I have been following this, and it makes perfect sense. However, I would like now to turn to the issues in the language, so that we might deal with this on another level. Specifically, I am wondering, how do we exegete Genesis 3:22 in the light of what has been discussed here?

> And the LORD God said, Behold, the man is become as one of us, to know good and evil: and now, lest he put forth his hand, and take also of the tree of life, and eat, and live for ever. (Genesis 3:22)

Also, the Spirit of Prophecy states this in the same terms:

> Adam and Eve were driven out of Eden, and **an angel with a flaming sword guarded the way to the tree of life**, that the disloyal, disobedient pair might not gain access to it and thus

immortalize transgression. Mark this point. The Lord did not place in Adam fallen and disobedient the confidence He placed in Adam loyal and true, living by every word that proceedeth out of the mouth of God. (White, *Christ Triumphant*, p. 26)

Demetrius: Man was to eat of the tree of life to maintain physical longevity, emblematic of an eternal existence through partaking of God Himself. In order to eat of the tree of the knowledge of good and evil, man had to first turn his back on the tree of life. Satan's suggestion to man was that he is his own god, independent of any outside source to maintain both his physical life and moral insight.

And the serpent said unto the woman, Ye shall not surely die: For God doth know that in the day ye eat thereof, then your eyes shall be opened, and ye shall be as gods, knowing good and evil. (Genesis 3:4, 5)

Both Adam and Eve accepted Satan's thought and chose to exalt themselves above God. They in effect declared that by eating of the tree of knowledge, they had become self-sustaining and had no need to eat of the tree of life.

And when the woman saw that the tree was good for food, and that it was pleasant to the eyes, and a tree to be desired to make one wise, she took of the fruit thereof, and did eat, and gave also unto her husband with her; and he did eat. (Genesis 3:6)

When they disobeyed God, they did not understand what was going on. It must be understood that the mechanics of their existence was not as it had been. Prior to sin, they existed under the environment of glory. After sin, they existed under the environment of grace. Grace came into effect as soon as there was a sinner. They did not physically die because of the plan of salvation. They did not know this until later. As soon as there was sin, there was a Savior. Humanity was condemned in Adam but executed in Christ. "And all that dwell upon the earth shall worship him, whose names are not written in the book of life of the Lamb slain from the foundation of the world" (Rev. 13:8).

Under glory, Adam and Eve were able to communicate directly with God having no veil between. However, after sin, under grace, this was not possible. Because of their now-sinful condition, they were unable to hold direct communication with God. Rather than seeing God, they now heard His voice. "And he said, I heard thy voice in the garden, and I was afraid, because I was naked; and I hid myself" (Gen. 3:10).

At this time, Adam and Eve had no direct access to God. They also had no direct access to physical life, but they were still physically alive. This means that God had implemented a plan to sustain them outside of the physical tree of life. The plan of salvation under grace has a different arrangement than the plan of longevity and the works of righteousness under glory.

Since the arrangement under grace was already implemented, then mixed signals would be transmitted to allow the sinners to directly approach the tree of life. It would have been instant death to Adam to approach God in his sinful condition. That would have been instant death to the sinner as in the case of Uzzah (See 2 Samuel 6:6–7).

In mercy God veiled Himself and directed man to leave the garden with the intention to bring him again.

God communicated the plan to Adam before he left Eden. Constrained by conviction because of the gift of the Spirit under grace, Adam and Eve obeyed God's voice and left the Garden of Eden.

Genesis 3:24 says, "So he drove out the man." It should be noted that Christ was also driven by the Spirit of God into the wilderness.

Mark 1:12 says, "And immediately the Spirit driveth him into the wilderness."

Being driven by the Spirit does not involve force but acting willingly based upon conviction of the will of God.

[Note: When God issues a directive in this way, He arises with irresistible authority; His Word, if it says anything, including "Get thee hence," will produce the result intended. It is not a threat of violence, but it is compelling, causing flight. It is how Lucifer and the rebels were driven from the heavenly precincts; it is how Christ drove Satan from His presence and the money changers from the temple.[9]]

> Kevin: Okay, this is good, yet I am still not entirely clear on the matter of inspiration (both the Bible and Spirit of Prophecy) declaring the potential for man to eat of the tree of life, after the fall, and become an immortal sinner. From what you are saying, this is not actually a possibility, for it would be as Uzzah coming into the presence of God without a covering.
>
> Demetrius: In Luke 16:19–31, Jesus describes a conversation between persons who had died. There are many who take what is said here to be a literal account, rather than understand the principle Christ was seeking to teach.

In Genesis 3:5, Satan said, "For God doth know that in the day ye eat thereof, then your eyes shall be opened, and ye shall be as gods, knowing good and evil."

Notice what God said.

> And the LORD God said, Behold, the man is become as one of us, to know good and evil: and now, lest he put forth his hand, and take also of the tree of life, and eat, and live for ever. (Genesis 3:22)

God said that man had become as one of them. What does God mean? Did man really become like God? Absolutely not! Was man now in a place to determine for himself what is good and what is evil? Absolutely not!

---

[9] For detailed coverage of this phenomenon, see *Awesome God: Songs of His Power, Volume 1*, Chapter 6, "Warfare, It Is Called."

Therefore the entire passage must be understood in light of what Satan suggested, what man believed, and the lesson God was seeking to give.

Satan believed that, by eating of the tree, man would become an immortal sinner. He figured that the tree was invested with the power to grant immortality. God knew differently. However God had a plan to give man immortality. Therefore, with the implementation of that plan, God diverted the man from every other plan that would have been destructive to him.

Hence, the language used must be understood within the principles of truth. If we carefully examine Genesis 3:22, and take it as it reads, without correctly applying right principles, we must then admit that God here declared that Satan was right in his assertions, that man actually became like God, that he was empowered by the tree to know good from evil, and that the tree was the means of maintaining his immortality and wisdom. If we accept that as a fact, then we must also accept that God recognized that Satan was right and He was wrong; and in order to prevent man from experiencing what Satan suggested, then He must take forceful, arbitrary measures to ensure that man does not have that experience. He actually cut man off from experiencing eternal life and godlike wisdom by cutting short his existence in inhibiting him from eating of the source of life. On the contrary, God's aim was to reconnect man to life and wisdom; therefore, He had to connect man to Himself Who is the Way, the Truth, and the Life.

> *God's aim was to reconnect man to life and wisdom; therefore, He had to connect man to Himself Who is the Way, the Truth, and the Life.*

Another principle to be observed is the one spoken of by Paul in Hebrews: "And almost all things are by the law purged with blood; and without shedding of blood is no remission" (Heb. 9:22).

Blood has to be spilled. This means that the sinner must die. But God wanted the sinner to live. Therefore God knew that the way for the sinner to live was not through his own efforts by laying hold on the literal, physical, earthly tree of life but by acceptance of the One Who has done it for Him.

Man has now the opportunity to lay hold of the tree of life and live in Christ. As a matter of fact, from the time Adam sinned, man was able to lay hold of the tree of life, not through his own effort but through the One Who has done it for him. The angels were placed there to distract man from the physical tree to the spiritual tree.

Those statements then must be taken within the context of the principles of redemption. Standing alone they will give an incorrect idea of God's intent.

> Kevin: Hmm. Deep stuff. The language issues are everywhere in Scripture, aren't they? And Satan stands by to inject meaning according to carnal understanding, which humans are so conditioned and accustomed to apply.

Here's something interesting. Notice this secret society symbol of the "Skull and Bones" fraternity with its reference to the passage in Genesis that we have been looking at:

Also Ellen G. White falls right in line with usage of the language, even though she gives strong keys to understanding the issues in the character of God. She even said:

> More and more I shall present the message to the people in Scripture language. Then if exception be taken by anyone, his contention must be with the Bible. (Letter 244, 1906)

This has been an excellent and profitable discussion. Thanks, Demetrius, for taking it up.

Part II: Afterthoughts: Dealing with the Spirit of Prophecy Statements

[This section is a discussion between D. Leach and K. Straub.]

Kevin: As with Scriptures, it is difficult sometimes to reconcile Spirit of Prophecy statements with what is really going on behind the scenes. I have been uneasy on this topic in terms of reconciling these excellent conclusions drawn from Scripture with the E. G. White narrative asserting that "Man was dependent upon the tree of life for immortality, and the Lord took these precautions lest men should eat of that tree 'and live forever'—become immortal sinners" (White, *Testimonies to Ministers and Gospel Workers*, p. 133). We have taught that we are dependent on God for our life, but inspiration appears to be conclusively stating that man had to eat this fruit to maintain immortality. Of course the source of life is God, but it was given through the partaking of this physical fruit.

Demetrius: Ellen White says this,

> After the entrance of sin, the heavenly Husbandman transplanted the tree of life to the Paradise above; but its branches

> hang over the wall to the lower world. Through the redemption purchased by the blood of Christ, we may still eat of its life-giving fruit. (*Heaven*, p. 172)
>
> Of Christ it is written, "In him was life; and the life was the light of men." He is the fountain of life. Obedience to Him is the life-giving power that gladdens the soul. (Ibid., p. 173)

She also said that the angels had something that had the appearance of a glittering sword. We must read between the lines.

> But holy angels were sent to drive them out of the garden, and to bar their way to the tree of life. Each of these mighty angels had in his right hand **something which had the appearance of a glittering sword.** (White, *Early Writings*, p. 148, emphasis added)

Through redemption, we can eat of its life-giving fruit. When was redemption instituted? Whenever that was, it was then that the tree was transplanted. This transplantation has to do, not so much with the removal of the tree on earth—even though there is a statement that suggests that—but *a transplantation of focus relative to access to God Himself, which is only through Christ*.

I also believe that in Sister White's mind, there was a development of thought on the issue and a clarification of terms used over the years with exposure to greater light.

Therefore, we need to put together all that she has written and see a principle arising rather than being bound by one statement. The Bible did say angels *and* a flaming sword. It is natural to understand angels with a flaming sword in their hands. However, the sword usually comes out of the mouth as in the case of Christ in Revelation 1:16.

Kevin: There may be many who would say, "Hold on, it isn't all that easy." Here again is the statement you provided,

But holy angels were sent to drive them out of the garden, and to bar their way to the tree of life. Each of these mighty angels had in his right hand something which had the appearance of a glittering sword. (White, *Early Writings*, p. 148)

If we were to ask the Spirit of Prophecy to answer these questions:

1. Why were the angels sent? Give two reasons.
2. What did the angels hold?
3. Where was that item held?

What would be the answers, based upon the text?

1. Drive them from the garden and keep them from coming back to eat from the tree of life.
2. Glittering swords.
3. In their right hands.

Demetrius: Okay. How does God bar the sinner from His presence? The revealing of the glory of God itself would present problems to the sinner. Even Moses was covered with the hand of God, hidden in the cleft of the rock.

Note in the case of Zechariah. God said that Jerusalem will be a city without walls. Yet He said that He would be a wall round about her. No sinner would be able to penetrate that wall because they would be consumed by their own unfitness. That is the everlasting burning of His presence.

> And, behold, the angel that talked with me went forth, and another angel went out to meet him, And said unto him, Run, speak to this young man, saying, Jerusalem shall be inhabited *as* towns without walls for the multitude of men and cattle therein: For I, saith the LORD, will be unto her a wall of fire round about, and will be the glory in the midst of her. (Zechariah 2:3–5)

Note this statement.

> The Garden of Eden remained upon the earth long after man had become an outcast from its pleasant paths. The fallen race were long permitted to gaze upon the home of innocence, their **entrance barred only by the watching angels. At the cherubim-guarded gate of Paradise the divine glory was revealed.** Hither came Adam and his sons to worship God. Here they renewed their vows of obedience to that law the transgression of which had banished them from Eden. When the tide of iniquity overspread the world, and the wickedness of men determined their destruction by a flood of waters, the hand that had planted Eden withdrew it from the earth. But in the final restitution, when there shall be "a new heaven and a new earth," it is to be restored more gloriously adorned than at the beginning. (White, *The Adventist Home*, p. 539, emphasis added)

Note that sentence, "At the cherubim-guarded gate of Paradise the divine glory was revealed." What was the glittering sword? The glory of God.

> Kevin: Good. Therefore we can see that there was a kind of Shekinah there, the presence of God, which cannot be approached by sinners or they will die. Therefore, an intercessor is required, and why they came there to worship through the sacrificial rite, utilizing an altar and a living animal, representing the Savior slain from the foundation of the world.

We should be consistent in our view of Genesis 3:22, as a reiteration of the thought presented to Eve by Satan, which she accepted, that they would become as gods, which included the concept of eternal life, which could be maintained at the tree of life while also eating of the forbidden tree.

Today's apostate religions propose the same. Isaiah 4:1 demonstrates that all religions of the world function under this paradigm.

Demetrius:

> Adam ate of the tree of the knowledge of good and evil, **the fruit of which he had been forbidden to touch**. His transgression opened the floodgates of woe upon our race. (White, *Heaven*, p. 172, emphasis added)

Was it true that God has said that they should not touch of the fruit? Notice Ellen White's progression of thought that, if not rightly understood, we would say that she contradicts herself and is therefore a false prophet.

> Eve had overstated the words of God's command. He had said to Adam and Eve, "But of the tree of the knowledge of good and evil, thou shalt not eat of it: for in the day that thou eatest thereof thou shalt surely die." **In Eve's controversy with the serpent, she added "Neither shall ye touch it."** Here the subtlety of the serpent appeared. This statement of Eve gave him advantage; he plucked the fruit and placed it in her hand, using her own words, He hath said, If ye touch it, ye shall die. You see no harm comes to you from touching the fruit, neither will you receive any harm by eating it. (White, *Confrontation*, p. 14, emphasis added)

In the first statement, there was a casual understanding of what went on in the garden where the focus was not on eating or touching but on the act of transgression. In the second statement, she is now being incisive in her exposition as she delves into the subtlety of the Serpent's statement.

> And the LORD God said, Behold, the man is become as one of us, to know good and evil: and now, lest he put forth his hand, and take also of the tree of life, and eat, and live for ever. (Genesis 3:22)

What does this phrase mean *"to become as one of us"*? Would not God want us to become like Him? Certainly. However, there is a way in which we can never become as God and continue to live. "Knowing good and evil" indicates that we can decipher for ourselves what is right and what is wrong. The Bible says that the way of a man is right in his own eyes. Hence, such a person claims himself to be god, not needing anyone, including Jehovah, to direct his path. When this occurs, God must in justice allow that man to prove his case.

> Produce your cause, saith the LORD; bring forth your strong [reasons], saith the King of Jacob. Let them bring them forth, and show us what shall happen: let them show the former things, what they be, that we may consider them, and know the latter end of them; or declare us things for to come. Shew the things that are to come hereafter, that we may know that ye are gods …. Behold, ye are of nothing, and your work of nought: an abomination is he that chooseth you. (Isaiah 41:21–24)

It was God's intention for man to put forth his hand and take of the tree of life and live forever, even after sin. However, the method for this to occur in justice would be through the plan of salvation. It is only *in Christ* that man can find again the path to the tree of life. The path to the tree of life was lost to man in Adam forever. The path to the tree of life is secured in the Second Adam.

There are things that God prohibits certain individuals to perform. Saul was prohibited from offering the sacrifice. That was the role of the priest. Why? The king needed to understand his dependence upon God and the system He had put in place as a safeguard for the king and his kingdom. Saul circumvented that plan and lost the kingdom.

We can therefore conclude that when all the statements from the Bible and Spirit of Prophecy are considered, within their rightful place, a beautiful principle of God's character emerges. God works with us at the level of our understanding. He understands our personal limitations, even misconceptions, and uses them to bring before us more clearly the truths of His Kingdom. We can trust God that regardless of the language used and how we may not fully understand those issues, His intention for us is only life and happiness. Let us therefore trust our God Who only has immortality, Who is the only One with the wisdom to direct our lives, and Who is the only One to provide for our every need.

CHAPTER 7

The Korah Rebellion: Destroyed of the Destroyer

"I was shown that the judgments of God would not come directly out from the Lord upon them but in this way:
They place themselves beyond His protection.
He warns, corrects, reproves, and points out the only path of safety; then if those who have been the objects of His special care will follow their own course independent of the Spirit of God, after repeated warnings, if they choose their own way, then He does not commission His angels to prevent Satan's decided attacks upon them."
White, *Manuscript Releases*, Vol. 14, p. 3

I've been looking at Paul's reference to the destroyer in 1 Corinthians 10:10. "Neither murmur ye, as some of them also murmured, and were **destroyed** of the **destroyer**" (emphasis added).

In addition to Paul's reference to the destroyer by name, there are three other direct references to him in the Scriptures.

In Exodus 12:23, we read:

> For the LORD will pass through to smite the Egyptians; and when he seeth the blood upon the lintel, and on the two side

posts, the LORD will pass over the door, and will not suffer the **destroyer** to come in unto your houses to smite you. (emphasis added)

In the Psalm 17:4, we read:

Concerning the works of men, by the word of thy lips I have kept me from the paths of the **destroyer.** (emphasis added)

And in John's Revelation, using the Hebrew and the Greek names meaning "destroyer," we read:

And they had a king over them, which is the angel of the bottomless pit, whose name in the Hebrew tongue is **Abaddon**, but in the Greek tongue hath his name **Apollyon.** (Revelation 9:11, emphasis added)

We will come back to 1 Corinthians later. First, I would like to have a little discussion on the Bible language and destroying angels.[10]

Evil Angels and Holy Angels Both Destroy

It is true that there are references to destroying angels that are from the Lord. These angels can be described as evil angels or as holy angels:

1) EVIL ANGELS. God gives over to free choice and then the forces of evil and demons come in to do their work, which is a work that always tends to destruction.

As an example, we have the classic case of Job, where Satan challenged God:

---

[10] A full study on this topic is available in *Awesome God: Songs of His Power, Volume I*. Each chapter in these two volumes of *Awesome God* is intended as a stand-alone read, so if the reader is good with this subject, jump ahead in this chapter to the discussion of 1 Corinthians 10:10.

> But **put forth thine hand** now, and touch all that he hath, and he will curse thee to thy face. And the LORD said unto Satan, Behold, **all that he hath is in thy power**; only upon himself **put not forth thine hand**. So Satan went forth from the presence of the LORD. (Job 1:11–12)

> While he was yet speaking, there came also another, and said, The **fire of God** is fallen from heaven, and hath burned up the sheep, and the servants, and consumed them; and I only am escaped alone to tell thee. (Job 1:16)

When we read in verse 11, the voice of Satan is speaking to God saying, "put forth thine hand now, and touch all that he hath," he knew that God was not going to do that, but that he was going to bring the action by his own hand. However, he was aware that in order to do so he needed permission from God. That is why we see in verse 12 that God said, "Behold, all that he hath is in thy power; only upon himself put not forth thine hand." The principle of God's permission is *always* the "active" agency. Destruction is never God's direct activity through holy angels, even though the text is formulated to read exactly that way, according to ancient Hebrew thought, their concept of Deity, and their general mode of expression, which we call the "major voice" of Scripture regarding God's wrath. That is, in many cases, the language portrays the evil as though it were done by God or by an evil angel or angels seemingly directly *sent* by God.

Examples:

> Then **God sent an evil spirit** between Abimelech and the men of Shechem; and the men of Shechem dealt treacherously with Abimelech. (Judges 9:23, emphasis added)

This one sounds like a holy angel was sent to do evil:

> And **God sent an angel** [God's Own holy messenger angel] [unto Jerusalem to destroy it: and as he was destroying, the LORD beheld, and he repented him **of the evil** [which is the work done

by evil angels as God permits through the holy angel messenger calling off restraints on evil angels and human passions] and said to the angel that destroyed, It is enough, stay now thine hand. (1 Chronicles 21:15, emphasis added)

God does not create evil, although the language of the Bible says He does (see Isa. 45:7). We must interpret the language to understand HOW He creates evil, then we can say along with the Bible that He creates evil. In the same way, holy angels do not work evil, only righteousness. But the Bible says they do work evil, so we have to find out how this happens, so that we can agree with the Bible and harmonize all of the references of violence and killing attributed to God with the reality of His non-violent character. The language need not be confusing once we understand the principle involved.

The following references seem to say that God commands evil angels and they follow God as their captain:

> But the spirit of the LORD departed from Saul, and an **evil spirit from the Lord** troubled him. (1 Samuel 16:14)

> He [God] cast upon them the fierceness of his anger, wrath, and indignation, and trouble, by **sending evil angels** among them. (Psalm 78:49, emphasis added)

Demonic forces do not work in obedience to God. Demonic forces work only to bring destruction. God's angels work only to benefit humans and part of this work consists in *restraining* destructive forces. Yet, they may also cease to perform their duties by *releasing* the powers of evil and chaos. That is the simple principle behind the language. So, when the text says God's angel was destroying, we can know that this is shorthand for stating that God's commanding angel came to tell holy angels to stand down and let the devil's forces do their work. When the text says that God commanded the destroying angel to cease, it is describing a command from God through His commanding angel down to His own forces

> *God's angels work only to benefit humans and part of this work consists in restraining destructive forces. Yet, they may also cease to perform their duties by releasing the powers of evil and chaos.*

to step in once again and restrain the forces evil.

We must stress, however, that all destruction is not of direct demonic activity. God can withdraw protective forces from nature itself without the direct involvement of demons. The classic example of this is the Flood (see Gen. 7:11; cf. Isa. 54:8, 9).

2) HOLY ANGELS. God gives over to the forces of evil, and demons come in to do the work, a work that always tends to destruction.

No, this is not a typo. It is the same thing operating in both cases and our explanation of it is the same explanation.

The angel of the Lord is cited as the destroying agent as punishment for David's sin of taking a census, as it is said, "And *Satan* stood up against Israel, and provoked David to number Israel" (1 Chron. 21:1).

> So Gad came to David, and said unto him, Thus saith the LORD, Choose thee Either three years' famine; or three months to be destroyed before thy foes, while that the sword of thine enemies overtaketh thee; or else three days the sword of the LORD, even the pestilence, in the land, and the **angel of the LORD destroying** throughout all the coasts of Israel. Now therefore advise thyself what word I shall bring again to him that sent me. (1 Chronicles 21:11, 12)

How did "the angel of the LORD" destroy? "So the LORD sent pestilence upon Israel: and there fell of Israel seventy thousand men" (1 Chron. 21:14). Now, bear in mind that this same story is told in 2 Samuel 24:1: "And again the anger of the LORD was kindled against Israel, and *he* moved David against them to say, Go, number Israel and Judah."

We noted above that 1 Chronicles says that it was *Satan* that incited David to number Israel. So, the lines are really blurred, aren't they?

We purposefully put this incident from 1 Chronicles 21 under the examples of evil angels sent to works of destruction, and here we are working with it under the examples of holy angels sent to works of destruction. The resolution to this matter, again, is to understand that holy angels are the ones controlling the forces of evil and chaos and, in the same way as the *Lord* is depicted in language as *doing* that which He *allows*, so are we to understand the language in reference to angels; they are represented at times as *executing* the destruction, when what is really happening is that they are *standing down* in their role of protecting, ministering spirits to men.

Another example is that of the slaying of the Assyrian army:

> And it came to pass that night, that **the angel of the LORD** went out, and smote in the camp of the Assyrians an hundred fourscore and five thousand: and when they arose early in the morning, behold, they were all dead corpses. (2 Kings 19:35)

Historical as well as inspired accounts point to this destruction, again, as being of a pestilential nature.

> Then the angel of the LORD went forth, and smote in the camp of the Assyrians a hundred and four score and five thousand: and when they arose early in the morning, behold, they were all dead corpses. (Isaiah 37:36)

> Age, position, or influence cannot save one of us from **sudden sickness and calamity** if the Lord says, "It is done." (White, *Manuscript Releases*, Vol. 16, p. 17)

Josephus, the Jewish historian to whom we refer as being authoritative in matters of antiquity, quotes Berosus, a Hellenistic-era Babylonian writer:

> Now when Sennacherib was returning from his Egyptian war to Jerusalem, he found his army under Rabshakeh his general in danger [**by a plague,** for], God had sent a **pestilential distemper** upon his army: and on the very first night of the siege, an hundred fourscore and five thousand, with their captains and generals, were destroyed. So the King was in a great dread and in a terrible agony at this **calamity**; and being in great fear for his whole army, he fled with the rest of his forces to his own Kingdom, and to his city Nineveh. And when he had abode there a little while, he was treacherously assaulted, and died by the hands of his elder sons, Adrammelech and Sarasar: and was slain in his own temple, which was called Araske. (Josephus, *Antiquities of the Jews,* Book X, Chapter 1.5 [accessed Nov. 30, 2022])

Remember the destruction of Jerusalem in AD 70, which we will cite from this statement in the inspired account of the Spirit of Prophecy:

> That magnificent structure [the temple] fell. **Angels of God** were sent to do the work of destruction, so that one stone was not left upon another that was not thrown down. (White, *Manuscript Releases,* Vol. 21, p. 66)

In this story, we have a most definite view as to the physical causation. History, as well as the Bible and Spirit of Prophecy narratives, tell us that it was the unmitigated passion and greed of the Roman army under Titus who razed the temple and the city.

Conclusion to the Section "Evil Angels and Holy Angels Both Destroy"

In essence, it does not matter whether the inspired text says that God sent evil angels to destroy or whether it says an angel of the Lord, or even Christ Himself—as in the case of Joshua and Jericho, where we find the "captain of the Lord's host" with sword drawn (Josh. 5:13–15)—the principal action is ever the same. God does not change. His actions are grounded in righteous principles, which are not variable. The language has variation, but not the principles of divine action. He does not pick and choose between using evil angels or holy angels to do the "evil" that befalls the wicked in judgment. Holy angels are always on a holy mission and, when destruction happens, it is an evil outcome due to an evil cause. Righteousness never works evil, although the Bible language at times appears to depict the righteous God sending evil. We must rightly interpret *how* it does this, so that we too can agree with the Bible, seeing that there is such a thing as *righteous evil*, as we recognize the function of figurative language that is informed by ancient Mesopotamian (Babylonian) culture.[11]

Destruction is the result of sin and separation from God and His ways. It is not the result of God's activity in any way, other than His active efforts to bring us salvation that we then reject. Then, the forces created by God, operating outside of God's control, are simply the natural consequences of our own choices. God's protections against destroying forces are not protections against Himself! This would be schizophrenic. To believe this, is to believe that God says to us, "I am your Saviour from the destroyer. But if you don't let me be your Saviour from the destroyer, I will destroy you." This is a most glaring *cognitive dissonance*.

Resuming the Discussion of 1 Corinthians 10:10

So then, coming back to Paul's reference to the destroyer in 1 Corinthians 10:10, we have some significant observations to make. Paul lists three of the Old Testament stories in which destruction came upon the rebellious.

First, there was the case of the newly emancipated slaves along with the Egyptian mixed multitude who, steeped in their original idolatry

---

[11] There is a chapter on this topic in *As He Is* which readers of *Awesome God* are encouraged to read as a primer to these studies.

and growing weary of waiting for Moses to come back from His encounter with God in the mountain, clamored for their old ways and committed sin:

> Neither be ye idolaters, as were some of them; as it is written, The people sat down to eat and drink, and rose up to play. Neither let us commit fornication, as some of them committed, and fell in one day three and twenty thousand. (1 Corinthians 10:7–8)

Next, there was the case of the people murmuring against God about their food and water and the venomous serpents coming out to bite them: "Neither let us tempt Christ, as some of them also tempted, and were destroyed of serpents" (1 Cor. 10:9).

We could examine these first two incidents listed by Paul in 1 Corinthians 10 for what they would teach us about God's methods, but here we want to focus in upon the third story. What incident is Paul referring to here? We quoted it at the beginning; let us quote it again now: "Neither murmur ye, as some of them also murmured, and were **destroyed of the Destroyer**" (1 Cor. 10:10, emphasis added).

Is this reference to murmuring alluding to either or both of Paul's first two examples? In principle, it could be both, but in consideration of the progression of thought and literary device, we are looking at a listing of separate incidents. Where do we find specific murmuring that results in destruction of the destroyer?

Theologians have been divided over which "murmuring" incident is referenced here. The *Seventh-day Adventist Bible Commentary* does not commit to either, but says:

> Two instances of murmuring followed by death are noted in the OT, the one in connection with the ten spies (Num. 13, Num. 14) and the other in connection with the rebellion of Korah, Dathan, and Abiram (Num. 16). (White, *The SDA Bible Commentary*, Vol. 6, p. 743)

Let us examine both stories.
1) **The Ten Spies.**
Some expositors go to Numbers, Chapter 14, at Kadesh, as the people quaked in fear at the report of the returning spies from the promised land:

> And all the children of Israel **murmured** against Moses and against Aaron: and the whole congregation said unto them, Would God that we had died in the land of Egypt! or would God we had died in this wilderness! And wherefore hath the LORD brought us unto this land, to fall by the sword, that our wives and our children should be a prey? were it not better for us to return into Egypt? And they said one to another, Let us make a captain, and let us return into Egypt. (Numbers 14:2–4)

God was about to wipe them out for this:

> And the LORD said unto Moses, How long will this people provoke me? and how long will it be ere they believe me, for all the signs which I have showed among them? I will smite them with the pestilence, and disinherit them, and will make of thee a greater nation and mightier than they. (Numbers 14:11–12)

But Moses interceded, remonstrating with God with razor sharp clarity, saying that it wouldn't present well on his character resume:

> And Moses said unto the LORD, Then the Egyptians shall hear it, (for thou broughtest up this people in thy might from among them;) And they will tell it to the inhabitants of this land: for they have heard that thou LORD art among this people, that thou LORD art seen face to face, and that thy cloud standeth over them, and that thou goest before them, by day time in a pillar of a cloud, and in a pillar of fire by night. Now if thou

shalt kill all this people as one man, then the nations which have heard the fame of thee will speak, saying, Because the LORD was not able to bring this people into the land which he sware unto them, therefore he hath slain them in the wilderness. (Numbers 14:13–16)

And so, Moses continued, asking the Lord to pardon them—which He *did*. The people who murmured were not specifically "destroyed of the destroyer" at this time.

However, the ten spies who brought a negative report died by a plague, Joshua and Caleb being spared. Their sin was not murmuring, however. Theirs was the sin of bringing an evil report from hearts of unbelief and faithlessness, from a reliance upon their own military might. Their sin was greater, in that they incited the people to murmur. So, they were given up to the natural consequence, to some undefined "plague." Perhaps something they picked up in the strange land. We are not often told what the pestilence was—it really is not important for us to know—yet, it is important that we understand that God, being cut off from the rebels, could only protect the two faithful ones.

Next, we find the people rebelling in another way, in that the Lord told them they would not go into the land. They decided that they would go in. They were warned against it, as Moses told them it was disobedience and "it shall not prosper" (Num. 14:41). Subsequently, left without the Lord's protection, they were wiped out by the Canaanites and the Amalekites.

These are separate incidents than the murmuring, so even though this is yet another time when the destroyer's work is manifest (for *all* destruction is ultimately the work of the destroyer), it is not the particular destruction referenced by Paul's phrase "destroyed of the destroyer." Paul's referent must be seen as a destruction effected as a direct result of murmuring. It is my opinion, based on the weight of evidence, that we must conclude that it would be forcing the interpretation of Paul's statement to refer to Numbers Chapter 14.

2) **The Korah Rebellion.**

Other Bible expositors turn to Numbers Chapter 16 to find a better fit, and there we will find all of the combined elements of murmuring and being killed by the angel of death (G3644 [ol-oth-ryoo-tace'] "olothreutes," or "a *ruiner*," that is, specifically, "a venomous *serpent*: destroyer.")

Here we see Korah, Dathan and Abiram with "two hundred and fifty of the princes of the assembly," coming against Moses and Aaron as rightful priests and leaders, claiming a right to minister in the sanctuary, asserting also that they are holy unto the Lord. Moses, after prayer, told them to come with their censers filled with their own fire and incense to minister before the Lord, and the Lord would show who have been chosen. Moses said to them, "For which cause both thou and all thy company are gathered together against the LORD: and what is Aaron, that ye **murmur** against him?" (Num. 16:11).

The men of Dathan and Abiram said to Moses,

> "Is it a small thing that thou hast brought us up out of a land that floweth with milk and honey, to kill us in the wilderness, except thou make thyself altogether a prince over us? Moreover thou hast not brought us into a land that floweth with milk and honey, or given us inheritance of fields and vineyards. (Numbers 16: 13–14)

So, at the time appointed, the defiant men came with their censers to the tabernacle. The entire congregation was present. The Lord told Aaron and Moses to run away because He was going to consume the whole lot, but Moses interceded with God to not be incensed with all of them solely on account of Korah. So God relented and told everyone to move away from the tents of ringleaders Korah, Dathan, and Abiram. Then Moses made a speech pertaining to the scene before them, saying basically that if nothing happens then God had not appointed Moses and Aaron, but if the ground swallows up the defiant ones, the people would have their answer. Then Moses' prophecy came true, and the people realized that the tents of these men were given up to the underground geological fault, causing what is commonly known as a sinkhole, and they, along with all their families and possessions, went down into the earth. The observing congregation was terrified and started fleeing the scene, afraid that they too might go down.

The next thing that happened was that there came out a "fire from the LORD" (keep in mind the "fire of God" mentioned in the story of Job, which was actually Satan's doing) and consumed the two hundred and fifty men who offered incense.

We would think that it was clear enough for everyone to see that testing the Lord was not a healthy thing to do, but no, the very next morning the congregation shows up. What do you think they were doing? "But on the morrow all the congregation of the children of Israel **murmured** against Moses and against Aaron, saying, Ye have killed the people of the LORD" (Num. 16:41).

Did they really think they could keep doing the same thing and expect different results? This is insanity!

> And the LORD spake unto Moses, saying, Get you up from among this congregation, that I may consume them as in a moment. And they fell upon their faces. And Moses said unto Aaron, Take a censer, and put fire therein from off the altar, and put on incense, and go quickly unto the congregation, and make an atonement for them: for there is wrath gone out from the LORD; the plague is begun. And Aaron took as Moses commanded, and ran into the midst of the congregation; and, behold, the plague was begun among the people: and he put on incense, and made an atonement for the people. And he stood between the dead and the living; and the plague was stayed. Now they that died in the plague were fourteen thousand and seven hundred, beside them that died about the matter of Korah. And Aaron returned unto Moses unto the door of the tabernacle of the congregation: and the plague was stayed. (Numbers 16:44–50)

In the analysis between the incidents at Kadesh (Numbers, Chapter 14) and here at the Korah rebellion (Numbers Chapter 16), we find, as above, that the specified destruction "of the destroyer," which one might expect for murmuring, was NOT executed against the people at Kadesh, whereas in the Korah rebellion, there were executions of the murmurers: first the leading men and their families, then the two hundred fifty princes, and then a sizeable portion of the general congregation.

Bible expositor Michael Shen concurs:

> Stronger evidence, however, supports Numbers 16. Paul's allusion suggests urgency, extensive danger, and immediacy in the punishment of death by "the destroying angel." In Numbers 14, the Lord "forgave" and stayed the execution of the unbelieving (Num. 14:20). Thus ... [some expositors] are "certain" that the Korah incident was in Paul's view (Num. 16:41). The decisive supporting evidence comes from Paul's use of ... [G622 (a-po'-loo-mee) "apollumi," "to DESTROY fully" (...to PERISH, or LOSE) ...], which establishes a clear word agreement with Numbers 16:33 ["they perished"] and 17:12 ["Behold, we die, we perish, we all perish]. The Korah incident also supports more cogently Paul's argument [which was for the Corinthians not to test the Lord when imposed upon by idolaters to make concessions against their faith]. (Li-Tak Shen, *Canaan to Corinth: Paul's Doctrine of God and the Issue of Food Offered to Idols in 1 Corinthians 8:1–11:1,* p. 71)

General Conclusion

Paul has given us a wonderful insight into the nature of the destruction that occurs against rebellion as that which comes when God gives over to the choice of the free moral agent who even goes so far as to declare his or her own holiness, in open defiance, even after having marked evidences of God's love and deliverance from bondage. When Paul identifies the source of the destruction as "the destroyer," we can know that it is not God nor holy angels who are directly responsible for the destruction and death that can and does occur. Note the linguistic connection in the word *destroyed* as Paul uses it in 1 Corinthians 10:10. The Greek "apollumi," reminds us of the Greek name given to the angel of the bottomless pit, "Apollyon" (Rev. 9:11).

We have three instances of destruction, recorded in Numbers chapter 16, that come upon the people as a result of murmuring. In every instance, there is a different mechanism. First, there is first a sinkhole for the main protagonists, then a lightning strike from the cloud of the Lord's presence for the immediate followers of those leading men, then a plague that begins to sweep through the general congregation, who also participated in the rebellion. The blame for these destructions is indiscriminately assigned to *"the destroyer"* which is unequivocally delineated in the Greek specifically as a *serpent*. The Bible defines the serpent, from Genesis to Revelation, as none other than Satan:

> And I **[God, speaking to the serpent]** will put enmity between thee and the woman [*Eve*], and between thy seed and her seed; it shall bruise thy head, and thou shalt bruise his heel. (Genesis 3:15, emphasis added)

> But I fear, lest by any means, as the serpent beguiled Eve through his subtlety, so your minds should be corrupted from the simplicity that is in Christ. (2 Corinthians 11:3)

> And the great dragon was cast out, that old serpent, called the Devil, and Satan, which deceiveth the whole world: he was cast out into the earth, and his angels were cast out with him. (Revelation 12:9)

In every case of the deaths that followed the Korah rebellion, Satan was the active agent. The first and third instances of death are in the realm of nature and the second instance, the "fire from the Lord" is what we

> *It is God that shields His creatures and hedges them in from the **power of the destroyer**.*

might deem as "supernatural" but the case is more likely that it is just as natural as the others, only we don't understand how it was produced.

The important thing is that we do not deviate from strict adherence to the principle that destruction comes when God gives over. Oftentimes, Satan has control of people and the situations they create because they have chosen him as another god. Sometimes, the enemy can exert his own direct power. In terms of biblical language, lightning generated by Satan would still be called "fire from the LORD. Other times people are given up to the warring elements of nature. Sometimes they are given over to wicked humans, whether others or themselves, and disease and death are the results.

We are told this:

> Therefore thus saith the Lord; Ye have not hearkened unto me, in proclaiming liberty, every one to his brother, and every man to his neighbour: behold, I proclaim a liberty for you, saith the Lord, to the sword, to the pestilence, and to the famine; and I will make you to be removed into all the kingdoms of the earth. (Jeremiah 34:17)

> Thus saith the LORD of hosts; Behold, I will send upon them the sword, the famine, and the pestilence, and will make them like vile figs, that cannot be eaten, they are so evil. And I will persecute them with the sword, with the famine, and with the pestilence, and will deliver them to be removed to all the kingdoms of the earth, to be a curse, and an astonishment, and an hissing, and a reproach, among all the nations whither I have driven them. (Jeremiah 29:17, 18)

Satan works through the elements also to garner his harvest of unprepared souls. He has studied the secrets of the laboratories of nature, and he uses all his power to control the elements **as far as God allows**. When he was suffered to afflict Job, how quickly flocks and herds, servants, houses, children, were swept away, one trouble succeeding another as in a moment. It is God that shields His creatures and hedges them in from the **power of the destroyer**. But the Christian world have shown contempt for the law of Jehovah, and the Lord will do just what He has declared that He would—He will **withdraw His blessings** from the earth and **remove His protecting care from those who are rebelling** against His law and teaching and forcing others to do the same. **Satan has control of all whom God does not especially guard**. He will favor and prosper some, in order to further his own designs; and he will bring trouble upon others and **lead men to believe that God is afflicting them.** (White, *The Great Controversy*, p. 589, emphasis added)

Finally, the implications of Paul's teaching in this passage are wonderful. We have a clear view to a proper understanding of numerous incidents in Scripture where people dropped dead, seemingly due to a direct strike from God.

- Uzzah? *Destroyed of the Destroyer*.
- Nadab and Abihu? *Apollyon*.
- The platoons of fifty that came to Elijah? *The Serpent*.
- Ananias and Sapphira? *You're getting it*.

May the name of the Lord be praised.

CHAPTER 8

The Babel Rebellion: When God Came Down to See

*"For God is not the author of confusion, but of peace,
as in all churches of the saints."*
1 Cor. 14:33

"For where envying and strife is there is confusion and every evil work."
James 3:16

It is a principle of the Divine government that nothing God does is arbitrary nor does He use physical force to obtain compliance from the rebellious or to execute punishment upon them for refusing Him the loyalty due Him. This can present a challenge in some Bible stories, as we look at the language which simply and matter-of-factly states, "God did it." Then we go to the Spirit of Prophecy for more clues and find more of the same. Ellen White wrote:

> More and more I shall present the message to the people in Scripture language. Then if exception be taken by anyone, his contention must be with the Bible. (Letter 244, July 17, 1906, par. 23)

Yet, like the Bible, we can find in the writings ample keys to define the character and attributes of God in matters of wrath and methods regarding His execution of warfare in the great controversy. A couple of short points are in order, that we might set the table to look briefly at what took place at Babel.

First, the language. The ancient near-Eastern view of deity attributed all things, good and evil, to the gods. The Hebrews were not any different in this. They adopted the mindset of the surrounding nations; and their view of God was also that He "brought" both life and death, light and dark, blessings and cursings. Their concept of an adversary or a great controversy was undeveloped. When Pharaoh hardened his heart against God, it was stated as though God had done it (Exod. 4:21; 7:2–13). When Saul committed suicide by the sword, it was portrayed as though God had slain him (1 Chron. 10:14). When the waters covered the earth and drowned the whole lot of them—save Noah's little band—it was God's genocidal plan for man and beast alike (Gen. 6:17). We smile at the apparent incongruity when we read that He was so angry that they were so violent that He would have to kill them all (Gen. 6:13).

In some of these stories, we find an actual cause for the destruction, pointing to the fact that God did not apply personal power, but that He gave the situation over to the forces of human wickedness, Satanic control, or natural chaos. He withdrew His protections and restraints. The Bible gives insight into this mechanism by using another Hebrew idiom, the "hiding of face." In that culture, the attitude of the face denotes favor and blessing or shunning and cursing. (Deuteronomy 31:16–18 spells it out.) In other stories, we are not given an etiological solution, nor any verbal indication of face-hiding, and we are left only with the bare language that apparently attributes a violent work to God. We need to get over that and just read it in the same way, whether an explanation is provided or not, instead of assuming that "sometimes" God really does project violent solutions to problems that He faces. Why do we have to make this assumption? Who says so? It is certainly not found anywhere in the Bible or Spirit of Prophecy. In fact, these both state otherwise. Ellen White, for example, gives a number of biblical references pertaining to the fires that burn up the wicked and then states categorically what those mean:

I will destroy thee ....

> This is not an act of arbitrary power on the part of God. The rejecters of His mercy reap that which they have sown. God is the fountain of life; and when one chooses the service of sin, he separates from God, and thus cuts himself off from life .... [The wicked] receive the results of their own choice. By a life of rebellion, Satan and all who unite with him place themselves so out of harmony with God that His very presence is to them a consuming fire. The glory of Him who is love will destroy them. (White, *The Desire of Ages*, 764)

That glory is not burning sheets of radiation that melt their eyes in their sockets, either. We have to get away from this kind of thinking. His glory is the revelation of His character. God destroys by trying to save. When His overtures are rejected, the results are a separation from Himself, which is a cessation of existence. The Spirit of Prophecy again makes it easy for us to understand:

> Let ministers and people remember that **gospel truth ruins** if it does not save. The soul that refuses to listen to the invitations of mercy from day to day can soon listen to the most urgent appeals without an emotion stirring his soul. (White, *Testimonies for the Church*, Vol. 5, p. 134, emphasis added)

Then, there is the related matter of a violent God Who just decides that it is time for Him to act, that the "cup is full" and that He can justifiably, according to righteousness, reach down and manipulate the situation to turn the great controversy in His favor. This is to say that God is arbitrary, in that He can just exercise His own discretion as He pleases, to build up or destroy, whatever the situation calls for, with no reference to anything but Himself. Those who believe this hide behind a senseless "sovereignty of God" argument. They will say, "He made it, He can destroy it. It belongs to Him. He can do with it as He pleases. They do not seem to think about the implications.

The flood is a classic example of this mode of thought. The kind of picture that the standard view of God's Character gives us is that God becomes suddenly concerned and sees that wickedness has become so great in the earth that He stands a good chance of losing every soul to the god of this world. Therefore, He must, at all costs, step in with power to ensure He does not lose the great controversy. If He did not do something drastic, He would have no human genetic line through which He might preserve the knowledge of Himself in the earth and bring forth His Son as the new Head of the race—no means whereby He might bring back righteousness and redeem mankind. So what to do? If you are all-powerful, it is easy. Quickly grab the few people who are still loyal, put them on a boat, and drown the rest! Does this make sense?

Satan started the great controversy by pointing to God as a cosmic control freak having laws in place to protect His position charging that His creatures were not truly free. So what would God be doing—if He were like this supreme being Who throws His weight around when the going gets tough—but proving Satan's contention? It simply does not add up. If God could just use His control over physics to manipulate any situation, there would be *no contest*. The controversy is *not* about who is more powerful physically. Satan knows the answer to that already. God knows it, too. Why don't *we* know it? The great controversy is about eternal divine principles versus independent creature ideology, and what constitutes true righteousness. In short, it is about God's character and government, and it is about how God goes about solving His problems, how He deals with disloyalty.

By the way, the Bible says something interesting about the flood, that should have corrected our thinking about this a long time ago:

> For a small moment have **I forsaken thee**; but with great mercies will I gather thee. **In a little wrath I hid my face from thee** for a moment; but with everlasting kindness will I have mercy on thee, saith the LORD thy Redeemer. For this is as the waters of Noah unto me." (Isaiah 54:7–9, emphasis added)

In Bible language, God "sent" the flood. In our western language and manner of thought, God withdrew His control from the elements as He departed from the antediluvians according to their own choice, and the results were disastrous, physically and literally:

> Hast thou marked the old way which wicked men have trodden? Which were cut down out of time, whose foundation was overflown with a flood: Which said unto God, **depart from us**: and **what can the Almighty do** for them? (Job 22:15–17, emphasis added)

True freedom, in God's government, means that He gives His subjects a choice while, at the same time, allowing the results of those choices to play out. God's "strange act" is exactly that. Oh, He has the power to save anyone from the results of bad choices, alright. He *can* do *anything*. If I smoke until my lungs are lumps of tar, He can give me new ones so I can ruin those ones, too. But this just makes Him a codependent, an enabler and perpetuator of the exercise of perverted desires. God does not do this. Instead, He patiently tries to save us from bad choices, even working with us within those choices, in ways to help extend our lives long enough to come around to Him and His ways. If He did not do this, not one of us would have survived long enough to be able to read and understand these words. This is called "permissive will," and it explains why God allowed ancient Israel to have eye-for-eye laws and why He gave them instructions in the use of the sword. God does not conduct war and justice like that. *Humans* do.

Leaving behind this brief primer, we now turn to our discussion to the events that happened at the Tower of Babel.

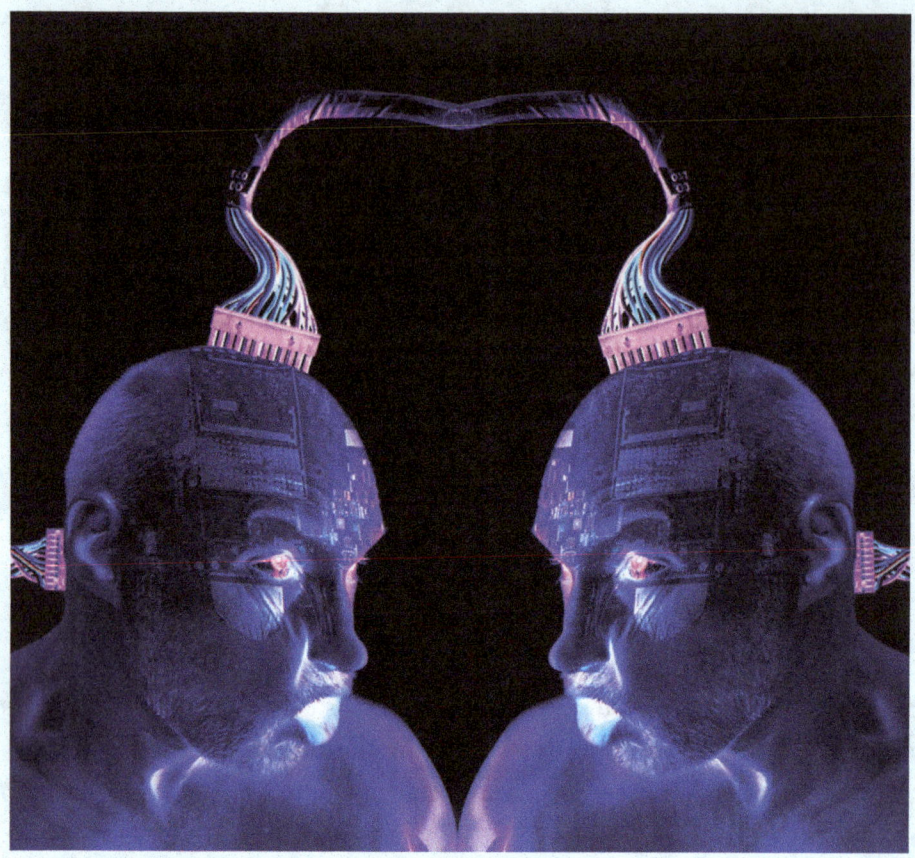

Did God see that things were again going badly for His cause and come up with a plan to thwart the evil designs of humans? He wouldn't kill them this time. That was really ugly and upon thinking about it, perhaps it gave Him a bad name. He would try something else. He would mess with their brains. This is what tradition teaches: God ruled over created beings as having no will of their own and much as a computer programmer would create and execute code, reached into the language centers of their brains and reprogrammed them. This, however, would be an arbitrary act, a discretionary exercise of divine power for the purpose of redirecting the current affairs of supposedly free moral agents. Suddenly and inexplicably, the language tree was birthed, and the various groups formed, each speaking precursory languages that would evolve into today's Japanese, French, Italian, German, English, and so forth.

I can remember listening to "The Bible in Living Sound" vinyl records as a child. The episode on the tower of Babel amused me to no end. As I would drop the phonograph needle on the record album, I would be taken back to that world: The builders were happily engaged in their monumental enterprise, calling up and down for bricks and mortar when, suddenly, the instructions were coming in a variety of languages, the foundation of the multiplicity of languages we have today. One fellow who still spoke English (!) exclaimed, "Has everyone gone crazy?" I would laugh heartily at the confusion of all that babbling on. The name *Babel* means "confusion," it is true, but the confusion comes not from God scrambling their brains to generate it, "for God is not the author of confusion" (1 Cor. 14:33). Confusion comes from man's envy, ambition, and desire for exaltation one over another (James 3:16). The situation only worsens as God withdraws, leaving the wicked to their own devices.

As Babel is a type of modern Babylon, the problem, from the divine point of view, is not primarily the language issue. It is not that the latter rebellion and confusion of false religions would be speaking the same literal language, or that they would overcome the language barrier—but that they would be speaking the same godless philosophies of man exalting self above God and seeking to save themselves by their own plans and methods, in defiance of the true God and *His* ways and commands. Allowing their plans to be broken up would slow them down, so that they would not fast-forward to extinction. In the antitype, we know that these builders of modern Babylon are once again moving inexorably toward the unity that was forged immediately after the flood. The inhabitants of earth are building the tower again, in their plans for a great "New World Order," now updated to "The Great Reset." The results will be the same. Just as in the type, the work will be making great progress, when suddenly the entire plan will come apart at the seams and the builders will turn on each other. We find through a study of the Bible and Spirit of Prophecy, that at the fifth plague, a "terrible awakening" (see White, *The Great Controversy*, p. 654) occurs and no longer will they speak the same language of support for Babylon. They will turn from blaming God for their calamities and realize that they have been fighting Him by persecuting those who would not go along with the New World Order and its false Sabbath. They then blame each other for their deceptions and such a slaughter will occur as has never before taken place. (This is the grape harvest under the sixth angel of Revelation 14:18–20; 19:15–21.)

> The schemes of the Babel builders ended in shame and defeat. The monument to their pride became the memorial of their folly. Yet men are continually pursuing the same course—depending upon self, and rejecting God's law. It is the principle that Satan tried to carry out in heaven; the same that governed Cain in presenting his offering.
>
> There are tower builders in our time. Infidels construct their theories from the supposed deductions of sciences, and reject the revealed word of God. They presume to pass sentence upon God's moral government; they despise His law and boast of the sufficiency of human reason. Then, "because sentence against an evil work is not executed speedily, therefore the heart of the sons of men is fully set in them to do evil" (Ecclesiastes 8:11).
>
> In the professedly Christian world many turn away from the plain teachings of the Bible and build up a creed from human speculations and pleasing fables, and they point to their tower as a way to climb up to heaven. Men hang with admiration upon the lips of eloquence while it teaches that the transgressor shall not die, that salvation may be secured without obedience to the law of God. **If the professed followers of Christ would accept God's standard, it would bring them into unity; but so long as human wisdom is exalted above His Holy Word, there will be divisions and dissension. The existing confusion of conflicting creeds and sects is fitly represented by the term "Babylon,"** which prophecy (Revelation 14:8; 18:2) applies to the world-loving churches of the last days. (White, *Patriarchs and Prophets*, pp. 123–124, emphasis added)

In the above passages, again we see that the lack of a language barrier was not really the issue. The issue was that they were building a tower in defiance of God. In this, they were seeking a unity apart from God, which is actually not possible. If God were to leave them to themselves, it would manifest very soon in violence. But in the case of Babel, something else happened—something astounding.

When we come to this narrative in the Bible, we have to look at it from the perspective of the principles of God's character and government, seeking to determine what could have happened there and why. We may not get all the answers, but we can certainly rule out some things, while gaining some valuable insights from various passages in inspiration as to why events transpired as they did.

Following are five criteria regarding God's conduct and other factors that must remain intact throughout the pursuit of an etiological solution to the confounding of languages at Babel. The big question here is, if it was not God that scrambled the people's language centers, then how did it happen?

1. Nothing God does in His conduct of the great controversy or His execution of judgment is an arbitrary act of power.
2. God does not use coercion to achieve His purpose. For God to proactively reprogram language centers of human brains to make them obey His command to spread out and populate the earth is an invasive procedure involving the use of force.
3. The biblical definition of divine wrath: God achieves His purposes and executes wrath and punishment by the principle of "giving over," or "Divine recession."
4. The results of Divine recession: "Giving over" means that the impenitent are given up to the forces and influences of carnal self, and/or demonic activity, and/or nature gone to chaos.
5. The narrative: The confounding of the Babel society through radical language alteration was a literal event, it occurred

instantaneously, and it produced comprehensible speech. The speech was split into various languages such as would be recognized only by others within the various groupings that were naturally formed by and due to this phenomenon.

Proof for the first four points is not needed, as it is expected that the reader will have gained this background from previous study. The fifth point is taking the Bible and the Spirit of Prophecy account at face value, as a supernatural, non-symbolic and non-evolutionary event.

God does not use coercion to achieve His purpose.

The Bible says that the Lord "came down to see the city and the tower" and noticed that the people were "one" and that they all had "one language" (Gen. 11:5–6). This was a problem, according to the way the story is presented. It implied that because of their ease of communication as a whole, they could all the more readily conspire freely against Him. Ellen White writes,

> Had this confederacy been permitted, a mighty power would have borne sway to banish righteousness—and with it peace, happiness, and security—from the earth. (*Patriarchs and Prophets,* p. 123)

So, He decided what to do about that.

> Go to, let us go down, and there confound their language, that they may not understand one another's speech. So the LORD scattered them abroad from thence upon the face of all the earth: and they left off to build the city. Therefore is the name of it called Babel; because the LORD did there confound the language of all the earth: and from thence did the LORD scatter them abroad upon the face of all the earth. (Genesis 11:7–9)

When God "came down" to inspect the situation at Babel, we are primed to read the narrative in an anthropomorphic sense. God didn't have to come down. He already saw it! In like manner, we must read the language of the Bible in this highly laconic story of the dispersion of the people as "God" confounding the language to create disunity, break up their political monopoly, and force them apart. As another way of looking at it in more modern terms, we could imagine God executing an anti-trust operation to break up the media establishment that Satan was building, because the people were all hearing the philosophies of their New World Order leaders in the same language. But God does not war in this way. He does not use carnal methods: God was seeing that the people had reached the saturation point of godlessness and that He would have to leave. He foresaw what would happen when He did that and this result is represented in the story as Him literally using His power to reprogram their brains, true to the major voice of the biblical narrative.[12]

> Earthly kingdoms rule by the ascendancy of physical power; but from Christ's kingdom every carnal weapon, every instrument of coercion, is banished. (White, *The Acts of the Apostles*, p. 12)

For God to force languages upon the people by reprogramming their brains is an act of overwhelming power using an "instrument of coercion." This would be unrighteousness. Yet, in righteousness, God gave them up to their choice to reject Him entirely, which allowed outside forces to go to work. He knew this would be the result. We can look to other events, such as the plagues in Egypt or the final plagues, and we can see that, in these also, God is not the active agent, but that He is giving over to outside forces. The destroyer that comes against the firstborn of Egypt is an evil angel (see Ps. 78:49). In the seven last plagues, likewise, the earth is given over to Satanic control:

---

[12] This topic is covered in detail in chapter four of *Awesome God: Songs of His Power, Volume 1.*

> The wicked have passed the boundary of their probation, and **the Lord withdraws his protection**, and leaves them to the mercy of the leader they have chosen. **Satan will have power** over those who have yielded themselves to his control, and **he** will plunge the inhabitants of the earth into one great, final trouble. As the **angels of God cease to hold in check the fierce winds of human passion**, all the elements of strife will be **let loose.** The whole world will be involved in ruin more terrible than that which came upon Jerusalem of old. (White, *The Spirit of Prophecy*, Vol. 4, p. 440.3, emphasis added)

Coming back to Babel, we find that the builders were gathered there in defiance of God. They were in unity on the matter, initially. However, some who were in support of the Babel system were God-fearing people who had been drawn into the scheme and did not yet understand what was happening. The Babel-builders and their pioneer followers' first course of action was to congregate in a city and establish human governance through kingly rule.

> Here they decided to build a city, and in it a tower of such stupendous height as should render it the wonder of the world. These enterprises were designed to prevent the people from scattering abroad in colonies. **God had directed men and women to disperse throughout the earth, to replenish and subdue it; but these Babel builders determined to keep their community united in one body, and to found a monarchy that should eventually embrace the whole earth.** Thus their city would become the metropolis of a universal empire; its glory would command the admiration and homage of the world and render the founders illustrious. The magnificent tower, reaching to the heavens, was intended to stand as a monument of the power and wisdom of its builders, perpetuating their fame to the latest generations. (White, *Patriarchs and Prophets*, p. 118, emphasis added)

The Babel Rebellion: When God Came Down to See

Instead of God creating the division, we find a principle embedded in the story that reveals rather that apostasy creates division.

> For a time the descendants of Noah continued to dwell among the mountains where the ark had rested. **As their numbers increased, apostasy soon led to division.** Those who desired to forget their Creator and to cast off the restraint of His law felt a constant annoyance from the teaching and example of their God-fearing associates, and after a time they decided to separate from the worshipers of God. Accordingly they journeyed to the plain of Shinar, on the banks of the river Euphrates. They were attracted by the beauty of the situation and the fertility of the soil, and upon this plain they determined to make their home. (White, *Patriarchs and Prophets*, p. 118, emphasis added)

They devised their plan to save themselves. Some wanted to figure out why the flood came without including any reference to God in the matter, according to false science. Others considered that this angry Deity could send another deluge and wanted to protect themselves. We find in this project a unity of both *atheists* and of "believers" *who had a wrong concept of God*:

> The dwellers on the plain of Shinar disbelieved God's covenant that He would not again bring a flood upon the earth. Many of them denied the existence of God and attributed the Flood to the operation of natural causes. **Others believed in a Supreme Being, and that it was He who had destroyed the antediluvian world; and their hearts, like that of Cain, rose up in rebellion against Him.** One object before them in the erection of the tower was to secure their own safety in case of another deluge…. And as they would be able to ascend to the region of the clouds, they hoped to ascertain the cause of the Flood. The whole undertaking was designed to exalt still further the pride of its projectors and to turn the minds of future generations away from God and

lead them into idolatry. (White, *Patriarchs and Prophets*, p. 119, emphasis added)

We must pause to note a very interesting point here and look critically at the ideas we have promoted about God's action at the flood. As we look about us in the Christian churches, including the Seventh-day Adventist Church, we must draw attention to the standard view. What do we believe about the flood? If we believe that the "Supreme Being ... destroyed the antediluvian world" we are speaking the same language as those whose "hearts, like that of Cain, rose up in rebellion against Him." This is a weighty matter! *Believing that God is actively genocidal leads to rebellion.* "But," the Bible student objects, "the Bible says God did it!" We reply, "Yes, it does. But how readest thou?" The Bible says it, *but what does the Bible mean*? We have to decode the language according to the keys that inspiration itself provides!

As the tower builders continued on with their plans, they came to a point where they passed the boundaries of their probation, and God gave them over. This principle can be found in yet another biblical key to explain divine wrath (Isa. 57:17). Note the definition of *wrath* in this text, which equates Divine "smiting" with the "hiding of face" principle. It is too clear to miss, when we break the text into its chiastic structure:

> A. For the iniquity of his covetousness
> > B. was I wroth,
> > > C. and smote him:
> > > C'. I hid me,
> > B'. and was wroth,
> A'. and he went on frowardly in the way of his heart.

God sees when men are so fixed in their rebellion that there is no more He can do to win them over. At this point, He gives them up to act without the application of His wisdom to guide them and/or restrain them and leaves them subject to forces that will destroy them. These forces, again, include carnal humanity, the demonic realm, and nature itself. As it is said, "Woe also unto them when I depart from them!" (Hosea 9:12).

Notice in the Isaiah 57:17 description of God's wrath, we start with a man who is given to covetousness. The outworking of God's "punishment," in this case, is to give him up to the same: he carries on in his own way, a way that leads to death. Paul also states the same principle: "And even as they did not like to retain God in their knowledge, God gave them over to a reprobate mind, to do those things which are not convenient" (Rom. 1:28).

So *to what* were those inhabitants on the plains of Shinar given up? They had disconnected from God and, when they reached their point of no return, the Spirit of God would have withdrawn and left them to their own choice to set up their own governance, entirely without reference to God. This would be the beginning of nations and politics. A. T. Jones writes much about the history of the world and, in particular, about the establishment of human governance by force of arms as having its inception at Babel. The Bible record of Nimrod is that "he began to be a mighty one in the earth;" or, as another translation gives it, "He was the first mighty one on the earth" (Gen. 10:8, AMPC).

That is, **Nimrod was the first one to establish the might, the power, the authority of human government in the form of an organised state.** He was the first man to assert the power and prerogatives, and assume the title, of king over men. "And the beginning of his kingdom was Babel, and Erech, and Accad, and Calneh in the land of Shinar" (Gen. 10:10).

Consequently,

> With the setting up of Nimrod's kingdom the entire ancient world entered a new historical phase …. His reign introduced to the world a new system of relations between the governor and the governed. The authority of former rulers rested upon the feeling of kindred; and the ascendency of the chief was an image of parental control. Nimrod, on the contrary, was *a sovereign of territory*, and of men just so far as they were its inhabitants, and irrespective of personal ties. Hitherto there had been tribes—enlarged families—Society: now there was a nation, a political community—the State. The political and social history of the world henceforth are distinct, if not divergent.

> **Such was the true origin of the state. It was the result of the apostasy of men from God.** Such only could possibly be its origin; for if all men had always observed the two "first of all the commandments," it would have been impossible for there ever to be any state. There could have been no human authority exercised. All would have been equally subject to God; He would have been the only Sovereign. (Alonzo T. Jones, "Society and the State, or the Origin of Civil Governments," *The Bible Echo*, p. 236, emphasis added)

Inspiration speaks to the principle of human politics leading to strife:

> God has warned his people not to become absorbed in politics. We cannot bear the sign of God as his commandment-keeping people, if we mingle with the strife of the world. We are not to give our minds to political issues. God's people are walking contrary to his will when they mix up with politics, and those who commence this work ... reveal that they are not taught and led by God, but by that **spirit which creates contention and strife and every evil work**. We are subjects of the Lord's kingdom, and we are to establish that kingdom in righteousness. (White, Letter 92, June 16, 1899, par. 12, emphasis added)

Abandonment of God leaves only the alternative of human politics, where striving for the mastery, for dominance over others, will be the foundation principle of human hearts.

> Love to God comprises our duty to God; love to our neighbor, our duty to one another. Mutual love must be cherished at all times, in all places, and under all circumstances .... This **love cultivated, becomes an abiding principle, and is effectual in rooting out dissensions and divisions** among brethren. **Where envying and jealousies are cherished**, there is every evil work .... Such a spirit is wholly in harmony with Satan, and is in

> accordance with his mind and purposes, fulfilling his will, doing his pleasure; for he knows **the sure result is separation from God.** ("Self-Exaltation," *The Review and Herald,* June 28, 1887, par. 7, emphasis added)

Satan would have two purposes at Babel. He desired to establish the state, where human governance would be institutionalized in monarchies and dictatorships, where people would be put into bondage to human governors and, through them, he would make it difficult to freely worship God with unhindered allegiance to the principles of His kingdom. Ultimately, he wanted to establish a one-world government right there at Babel, through which he could work to secure total domination over every soul. This has ever been his purpose. But he faces a serious difficulty in achieving this. With the weakening of restraints previously put in place by the Spirit of God, humans would be continually at war with each other, thereby frustrating his purpose to achieve the level of unity that would be required. However, at the same time, warring states are delightful to him. Thus we see in this story a conflicting set of motivations. All the resultant death and misery would secure souls to his side. Keeping nations perpetually at war could be used to the same end, but it would take more time. Through the system of nations and their rulers, God's kingdom would be nearly extinguished through secular humanism, idolatrous pagan religions, and atheism while he could work to bring about his great new world global coup d'état order against God in other ways.

> Satan delights in war, for it excites the worst passions of the soul and then sweeps into eternity its victims steeped in vice and blood. It is his object to incite the nations to war against one another; for he can thus divert the minds of the people from the work of preparation to stand in the day of God. (White, *Counsels on Health,* p. 460)

God gave up the inhabitants of Babel to that which caused the ruin of the human race before the flood.

The Flood cleansed the earth of the wickedness and violence that had cursed it to its ruin; and again mankind and the world were started with those who were willing to have God dwell with them to lead them in the way of light. But again there were those who loved darkness rather than light, and practiced the deeds of evil. Strife and violence grew until *force* became the only prevalent authority; and this *itself* developed the mighty imperial power of Nimrod. (Alonzo T. Jones, "Through the Bible—IV," *The Medical Missionary Articles (1903–1909),* April 15, 1908, pp. 311, 312)

So, as the building project progressed, the inhabitants of that tower and city rejoiced in their success, praising their idol gods as they had "set themselves against the Ruler of heaven and earth. Suddenly the work that had been advancing so prosperously was checked. Angels were sent to bring to naught the purpose of the builders" (White, *Patriarchs and Prophets*, p. 119).

> *Suddenly the work that had been advancing so prosperously was checked. Angels were sent to bring to naught the purpose of the builders*

Here is a curious statement that angels had something to do with what happened next. In Volume 1 of *The Spirit of Prophecy*, 1870, p. 92, Ellen White specifies "two angels." We have studied in other chapters to clarify the work of angels of destruction, showing how they work in accordance with how God works. If we see Jesus ever running a man through with a sword of steel, then we would see an angel doing likewise. If we ever see Jesus confusing or forcibly altering a man's mind, then holy angels would work in the same way. But this is not what we observe. We must see another principle at work, in that God does not actively move in to disrupt men or nature by the arbitrary exercise of the power that He possesses—and which He *could* wield in such a manner if it were in His character to do so.

As we have shown, God gives over to the ways that self has chosen. The role of angels is "to minister for them who shall be heirs of salvation"

(Heb. 1:14), which the messenger to the final generation confirms, when she says, "Angels are sent ... *not to destroy*, but to watch over and guard imperiled souls" (*Review and Herald*, May 10, 1906, par. 15, emphasis added). When the subject(s) of their ministry reach a point of fixed determination in rebellion, angels are instructed to relay orders to the front line sentinels to step aside from their saving and protecting role, and chaos is the result. This is how it can be said that "Angels were sent" to check the project of those builders. It is the same as we would find in other places, such as in the destruction of the temple at Jerusalem. There, we find the historical record showing that *the Roman soldiery* razed the temple with unmitigated greed and fury. Yet, even though The Spirit of Prophecy faithfully records it as it happened, we find again the usage of biblical language with reference to an apparent direct act of destruction by angels in that scene:

> [Man's expensive] ... buildings will share the fate of the temple in Jerusalem. That magnificent structure fell. Angels of God were sent to do the work of destruction, so that one stone was not left upon another that was not thrown down. (White, *Manuscript Releases*, Vol. 21, p. 66)

We can therefore even say that "angels of God" brought down the twin towers in New York City, or any natural or manmade disaster. All of such "acts of God" as they are labelled in human language, are in the biblical parlance attributed to the work of God's angels, yet not in the way we would normally understand from a surface reading of the language.

Returning to our story at the tower of Babel, we come to the point where the workers and their foremen had a grand structure partially erected but, due to the size of the structure, carrying forward the project was becoming more and more complex, especially regarding communications. As God withdrew from them, their language became inexplicably altered. Gross misunderstandings in communication were the result, creating extreme confusion. Frustration levels ran high, setting up conditions for strife that led to open violence and bloodshed.

> The tower had reached a lofty height, and it was impossible for the workmen at the top to communicate directly with those at the base; therefore men were stationed at different points, each to receive and report to the one next below him the orders for needed material or other directions concerning the work. **As messages were thus passing from one to another the language was confounded**, so that material was called for which was not needed, and the directions delivered were often the reverse of those that had been given. Confusion and dismay followed. All work came to a standstill. There could be no further harmony or co-operation. The builders were wholly unable to account for the strange misunderstandings among them, and in their rage and disappointment they reproached one another. Their confederacy ended in strife and bloodshed. (White, *Patriarchs and Prophets*, 119)

While they were working, passing messages up and down, their speech was altered. From all that we have explored so far, we might see some lines of reasoning that do not add up, according to the narratives. It might seem that simple miscommunications got out of hand through the distortions that came from relaying messages through numerous repeaters, and this is what led to warring factions which then dispersed. Or it could be suggested that the confusion of language was a rapid evolution of people groups who spoke not actual different tongues, but rather had different political and religious ideologies, which led to warring factions and dispersion. From these, we would see the people spread out over the earth to develop languages naturally. But the historian Josephus, who stays close to the biblical narrative, would not direct us to such conclusions:

> When God saw that they acted so madly, he did not resolve to destroy them utterly; since they were not grown wiser by the destruction of the former sinners: but **he caused a tumult among them, by producing in them diverse languages; and causing, that through the multitude of those languages, they should not**

be able to understand one another. The place wherein they built the Tower is now called *Babylon*: because of the confusion of that language which they readily understood before: for the Hebrews mean by the word *Babel, Confusion*. The *Sibyll* also makes mention of this tower, (21) and of the confusion of the language when she says thus: 'When all men were of one language, some of them built an high tower, as if they would thereby ascend up to heaven. But the Gods sent storms of wind, and overthrew the tower, and gave every one his peculiar language. And for this reason it was that the city was called *Babylon*. (Flavius Josephus, "Comparing the Tower of Babel, and the Confusion of Tongues," *Flavius Josephus of the Antiquities of the Jews,* Book 1, Chapter 4, par. 3, emphasis added)

The inspired account of Ellen White does not lend support to anything other than an actual disruption of speech:

Up to this time all men had spoken the same language; now those that could understand one another's speech united in companies; some went one way, and some another. "The Lord scattered them abroad from thence upon the face of all the earth." **This dispersion was the means of peopling the earth, and thus the Lord's purpose was accomplished through the very means that men had employed to prevent its fulfillment.** (*Patriarchs and Prophets*, 120, emphasis added)

With both history and inspiration speaking of a literal, instantaneous diversification of language without any suggestion that the scriptural account could have been rather an allusion to miscommunications getting out of hand or to a dispersion based on political or religious beliefs, we must conclude that by some means their language was truly altered.

So, what are we to conclude? Did God directly reprogram their brains? We do not accept that. Why? What is the particular problem with that conclusion? It is that it violates Divine principles. God does not exercise arbitrary power (White, *The Desire of Ages*, p. 764). Nor does He stand "as an executioner of the sentence against transgression" (White, *The Great Controversy*, p. 36).

The best etiological approach to this story is in the idea that angels were commanded to stand down in their protective role. So, what would that look like? What, or *who*, moved in when protective forces were taken out of the way? We will come back to this, shortly.

Notice especially this sentence: "This dispersion was the means of peopling the earth, and thus **the Lord's purpose was accomplished through the very means that men had employed to prevent its fulfillment**" (White, *Patriarchs and Prophets*, p. 120). In this, we find a clue as to what is happening in this story. *God's purpose* was to disperse them so that they would "go forth to found nations in different parts of the earth" and "carry with them a knowledge of His will, that the light of truth might shine undimmed to succeeding generations" (White, *Patriarchs and Prophets*, p. 120). *Their purpose* was to stand in defiance of God through science and through adherence to a philosophy of His character as tyrant-destroyer (see White, *Patriarchs and Prophets*, p. 119). The *means* that men employed was in rallying together on the plains to build a tower. How did God accomplish His purpose through their rebellion? This is the subject that inspired text is discussing. It would not make any sense at all if God were to force them to disperse against their will, in their rebellion, when He purposed to make them missionaries for His cause. His purpose was accomplished by letting them alone and letting Satan have his way with them. This should not surprise us, for God's purpose in the overall great controversy is accomplished in the same way. Satan is given enough rope to hang himself. God allows the rebellion to mature and, in that way, it will prove itself untenable.

Again, let's look at some of Josephus' telling of the Babel history:

> **God also commanded them to send colonies abroad, for the thorough peopling of the earth; that they might not raise seditions**

among themselves, but might cultivate a great part of the earth, and enjoy its fruits after a plentiful manner. But they were so ill instructed, that **they did not obey God. For which reason they fell into calamities**, and were made sensible by experience of what sin they had been guilty of. For **when they flourished with a numerous youth, God admonished them again to send out colonies**. But they imagining the prosperity they enjoyed was not derived from the favour of God, but supposing that their own power was the proper cause of the plentiful condition they were in, **did not obey him**. Nay **they added to this their disobedience to the divine will, the suspicion that they were therefore ordered to send out separate colonies, that, being divided asunder, they might the more easily be oppressed.**

Now it was **Nimrod who excited them to such an affront and contempt of God.** He was the grand-son of Ham, the son of Noah: a bold man, and of great strength of hand. He persuaded them not to ascribe it to God, as if it was through his means that they were happy; but **to believe that it was their own courage which procured that happiness. He also gradually changed the government into tyranny; seeing no other way of turning men from the fear of God, but to bring them into a constant dependence on his own power.** He also said, "He would be revenged on God, if he should have a mind to drown the world again: for that he would build a Tower too high for the waters to be able to reach; and that **he would avenge himself on God for destroying their fore-fathers.**" (Ibid., par. 1 and par. 2, emphasis added)

Note at the start of the Josephus text, he says that God intended to spread them out to avoid their starting uprisings and contentions amongst themselves. But they disobeyed God and instead concentrated themselves in a city. This hardened into such a defiant rebellion that God had to honor their choice and give them over. As in the plagues of Egypt, He sent "evil angels among them" (Ps. 78:49). This was done by a two-stage process: He sent holy angel messengers to instruct holy sentinels on earth to let the evil angels have their way. *The evil angels then went to work to confuse the people's language.* This led to strife among them to the point of violence and murder. We should not be alarmed at the bold assertion that evil angels then went to work to confuse their language, which seems to directly contradict Scripture when it says that *God* confused their language. This is Bible language, such as when God "put a lying spirit in the mouth of" false prophets (1 Kings 22:23).

One may argue that Satan could not possibly have this power over minds to perform such an intricate operation. But do not forget that he can do wonders when he is allowed to work.

> So far as his power extends, he will perform actual miracles. Says the Scripture: "He ... deceiveth them that dwell on the earth by the means of those miracles which he had power to do," not merely those which he pretends to do. Something more than mere impostures is brought to view in this scripture. (White, *Testimonies for the Church*, Vol. 5, 1889, p. 698)

Some might think that one act is just as arbitrary as another. God would not actively scramble their language and then, through the resultant confusion, bring about war and bloodshed. This is never His kind of work. Why then would God suddenly give them over to evil forces that would do this very thing? We must not underestimate the power of choice along with the power of prayer. These two things affect the efficacy and strength of His influence. Evil choices will push Him away and reduce His influence, while prayer brings Him near and allows Him to act on behalf of the supplicant's righteous desires. In all of this, the terms of the great controversy do not allow Him to use any of Satan's methods, but only ever to act in accordance with His own principles of righteousness.

> The men of Babel had determined to establish a government that should be independent of God. **There were some among**

> **them, however, who feared the Lord, but who had been deceived by the pretensions of the ungodly and drawn into their schemes.** For the sake of these faithful ones the Lord delayed His judgments and gave the people time to reveal their true character. As this was developed, the sons of God labored to turn them from their purpose; but the people were fully united in their Heaven-daring undertaking. (White, *Patriarchs and Prophets*, p. 123, emphasis added)

> **Those that feared the Lord cried unto Him to interpose** …. In mercy to the world He defeated the purpose of the tower builders and overthrew the memorial of their daring. In mercy He confounded their speech, thus putting a check on their purposes of rebellion …. From time to time the unseen hand that holds the scepter of government is stretched out to restrain iniquity. (White, *Patriarchs and Prophets*, p. 123, emphasis added)

Another question that then comes into all of this is "Why would Satanic forces go to work to diversify the languages when the result would be the fulfilment of God's purposes to disperse the people over the face of the earth?" Under restraint, the best that Satan could do was to have them concentrate in a city, build up their defiance of God and *then* go out to cover the world with rebellion, under a one world government. This was his purpose, as we noted earlier that "these Babel builders determined to keep their community united in one body, and to found a monarchy that **should eventually embrace the whole earth**. Thus their city would become the **metropolis of a universal empire**" (White, *Patriarchs and Prophets*, p. 118, emphasis added).

But once the restraint was lifted, Satan saw that he could achieve the following numerous objectives.

1) For the accomplishment of these goals, he was willing to sacrifice the present unity he apparently enjoyed, but which he did not actually have, as we have seen. He would have

known that he had a problem with this people group who yet remained connected to God. So, he would deal with them by cutting off their influence. He could not touch them, so they would remain in one group, retaining their original language. From Satan's perspective, it was better to have it so, keeping his "problem group" in one place.

2) He could cause "war and bloodshed," in which he delights (*Review and Herald,* September 17, 1901, par. 9). This objective would be achieved both in the short term, right here in the city, and in the long term, as nations would be established and go to war with one another.

3) He could spread the hardened and rebellious hearts throughout the world—hearts filled with the same principles of tyranny in government—and, through this means, continue to work his ultimate objective to bring about a world rule. In this context—and I'll leave the reader to ponder rather than delve into discussion of secret societies and the New World Order—it is interesting to note the statement by legendary Freemason Arthur E. Waite, saying, "As regards to Masonry, Babel of course represented a Masonic enterprise .... Out of evil comes good, however, and the confusion of tongues gave rise to 'the ancient practice of Masons conversing without the use of speech'" (*A New Encyclopedia of Freemasonry and of Cognate Instituted Mysteries: Their Rites, Literature and History*, Volume I). Embedded in this is the idea that God confounded the languages, in the words "out of evil comes good," for the evil here spoken is attributed to an act of God. It is that classic inversion of good and evil. The Babel builders and their society would have thought themselves on the side of freedom and righteousness, having their minds captive to the enemy of souls and chief liar, Satan, who was working through the master Mason, Nimrod.

> 4) Lastly, he could do this work and make it look as if God did it, continuing his propaganda program of blaming God for calamity.
>
> Satan has control of all whom God does not especially guard. He will favor and prosper some in order to further his own designs, and he will bring trouble upon others and lead men to believe that it is God who is afflicting them. (White, *The Great Controversy*, p. 589)

But why would Satan care about making such a trade-off? Why not just leave things alone and let the work continue? Why not secure the inhabitants of his city under total tyranny and eradicate any that defied his purposes? What was he afraid of?

First, he had seen that God protects His own. He could not touch them unless God allowed it. He would have to get to them in another way. For the time being, though, he could keep his own from hearing the truth and becoming converted. So, he confused their speech that they could no longer understand God's people. Do we have inspired evidence to support this idea?

> But at what loss to those who had set themselves against God! It was His purpose that as men should go forth to found nations in different parts of the earth they should carry with them a knowledge of His will, that the light of truth might shine undimmed to succeeding generations …. But they were unwilling to listen to these unpalatable truths; they had no desire to retain God in their knowledge; and **by the confusion of tongues they were, in a great measure, shut out from intercourse with those who might have given them light.** (White, *Patriarchs and Prophets*, p. 120, emphasis added)

Admittedly, the story of the confounding of languages at Babel is a difficult one. We have many instances of Bible language that say God did a thing but we know from the narrative itself that it wasn't actually a "doing" of God physically, but rather that other forces did the acting, which God allowed by not interfering. A classic example of this is seen in the well-known comparison of 1 Chronicles 10:14 with verse 10:4, regarding the death of Saul. In v. 14, it says "he [God] slew him" and in v. 4 says, "Saul took a sword, and fell upon it."

However, the Bible language issue is not the only obstacle in settling upon a plausible etiological solution. To attribute the confounding of languages to Satan requires us to overcome the difficulties of whether Satan would have the power to truly bestow permanent languages by physiologically rewiring the brain, removing the native language, and inserting a new language. It also requires us to deal with the question of why Satan would seemingly reverse his original objectives to confederate against God's intention to disperse. But what other conclusion can be made? To believe that God did this work, we would have to overcome the difficulty of denying it as an arbitrary and coercive act.

Some researchers have tried to avoid either conclusion by suggesting that an electromagnetic storm messed them up, but this would not create languages, but confusion only, as no affected individual would understand another. Though somewhat interesting, we have not even discussed any of those theories here, because the Spirit of Prophecy and other sources clearly indicate that people were divided into language groups, that could understand speech within their respective groups, and that were banded together along linguistic lines and dispersed from the plains on that basis. This is the inspired record and ancient historians confirm it.

Some people think that Satan could not do this miracle. We are told that he can do miracles when he is given permission, although we are not told what the extent of his abilities might be. We are left to assume that this is something he can do, when given the freedom to perform it. There are accounts of people suddenly forgetting their native language due to brain trauma and speaking new languages yet the basis for those new languages was established earlier in life. They had some previous exposure to the new languages and had forgotten them through disuse. There is the account of Therese Neumann of Germany (1898–1962), a Roman Catholic stigmatic who is alleged to have acquired miraculously the four languages spoken at the time of Christ—Latin, Hebrew, Greek and Aramaic. Scholars at the time who analyzed her use of these languages were convinced of their veracity:

These well-known scholars came to the conclusion and they stated it categorically that Therese's knowledge of these languages was absolutely correct, and that it was impossible for her knowledge to be explained by any falsehood or power of suggestion. Many other university professors who had similarly tested her came to the same conclusion. Dr. C. Wessely stated: **"Therese Neumann's knowledge of Christ's own language is a miracle in itself. I am amazed at her knowledge of Aramaic in particular"** ("The Supernatural Gift of Understanding Foreign and ancient Languages," Miracles of the Saints, https://1ref.us/stra6 [accessed Dec. 6, 2022]).

The reader can research this point, as to whether there might be any properly verified instances of permanent foreign language acquisition. It seems that it is likely, given the choices we are facing in explaining the power behind the confusion of languages in the Babel story. I think of the many examples we have of extraordinary individuals who through an accident of development, such as autism, have superlative gifts in music or math, "languages" in themselves, which emerge spontaneously from these minds at preschool ages never having learned, but demonstrating abilities far beyond the ordinary person with training. I am not saying Satan is behind the prodigy or the savant. What I am saying is that there are mechanisms that can be triggered that open the mind or endow the mind with incredible abilities. We can also read well-documented stories of people acquiring musical abilities through making a pact with demons. Obviously, evil beings can be given permission to work some fantastic effects on the mind.

It may seem strange to think that our languages have their origin in the god of this world, the fallen arch-rebel, Satan. Yet it is fitting, for this entire world is a Babylon, a confusion, not only of languages, but of political and religious ideologies and governments. At last, in the restoration, there will be no more division. God will heal that wound. In Bible language, what God has allowed to take place that brought confusion and bloodshed, He will actively intervene to correct. Both are represented as the activity of God: "See now that I, even I, am he, and there is no god with me: I kill, and I make alive; I wound, and I heal: neither is there any that can deliver out of my hand" (Deut. 32:39).

In this manner, we see the Bible language portraying God as the confounder of languages and again as the agency through which the confusion is dissolved. It is interesting to note that people speaking various languages became "confounded" when God brought unity of understanding through the removal of the language barrier through the outpouring of *His Spirit*, on the day of Pentecost: "Now when this was noised abroad, the multitude came together, and were confounded, because that every man heard them speak in his own language" (Acts 2:6).

> *Babel's diaspora will be reversed at the tree of life*

Babel's diaspora will be reversed at the tree of life:

> I then saw Jesus leading the redeemed host to the tree of life, and again we heard his lovely voice, richer than any music that ever fell on mortal ear, saying, The leaves of this tree are for the healing of the nations. (White, *Spiritual Gifts*, Vol. 1, p. 210)

CHAPTER 9

Abraham, Take Now Thy Son

"And Abraham said, My son, God will provide himself a lamb for a burnt offering: so they went both of them together."
Gen. 22:8

"And he made his grave with the wicked, and with the rich in his death; because he had done no violence, neither was any deceit in his mouth. Yet it pleased the LORD to bruise him; he hath put him to grief: when thou shalt make his soul an offering for sin."
Isa. 53:9–10a

"Jesus cried with a loud voice, saying, ... My God, my God, why hast thou forsaken me?"
Matt. 27:46

-----Original Message-----[13]
From: WP
To: Kevin Straub

---

[13] Note: The following study is taken from the author's work in online correspondence as a Bible worker, retaining that format of written communication. Some edits to the content have been made for clarity.

Subject: Abraham and Isaac
Tim Jennings recently did a blog on Abraham's attempted sacrifice of Isaac. *I have a different view on the story given the stance that God does not kill …

*[Note to reader: the view here is that Satan posed as God and gave the command to Abraham to offer his son as a burnt offering.]

Kevin Straub:

I believe we are obligated to take a different approach to this.

In some cases, I believe we can clearly make attribution to Satan, as in the destroyer of the firstborn in Egypt and in the destruction of the rebels during the Korah, Dathan, and Abiram uprising, and others. However, we must be careful not to contradict the inspired account that we have in the Spirit of Prophecy. The Messenger to the remnant clearly states that God gave the command to Abraham to "slay" Isaac (see Chapter 13, "The Test of Faith," in *Patriarchs and Prophets*) and Satan was even standing by, she says, to cause him to doubt that it was the command of God, because God's law says not to kill. But when he saw the "cloud of glory hovering over Mount Moriah," to signify which place he was to go, "he knew that the voice which had spoken to him was from heaven" (White, *Patriarchs and Prophets*, p. 151). What is going on with this? You are correct in saying that if we received such a command in our present times we would surely be saying "Get thee behind me, Satan," or, if certain we were being spoken to by God, we would be asking Him to interpret what He meant by that, knowing that He doesn't kill anyone and will never ask us to kill anyone. We would not take our son to the mountain thinking to offer a human sacrifice. We know that we would not have any lesson to learn in symbol regarding God's sacrifice of His Son because that has already been done and we have the record of it. We also understand that our Redeemer has died and risen again. But Abraham did not know what this was all about until his hand was stayed and God provided a ram in Isaac's stead.

It is a difficult story to reconcile. God gave a command that ran counter to a command. God, knowing the end from the beginning, knew that He would not require it to be carried out at last, for that would not be righteous, but that He did require Abraham's willingness to carry it out, and *that* was righteous! I can only conclude that God was doing this to allow Satan to severely test Abraham, as in the Job story. Satan was accusing Abraham "of having failed to comply with the conditions of the covenant and therefore as unworthy of its blessings." So, God put Abraham to the test to expose Satan in regard to the bigger issues in the great controversy, as a spectacle to the universe. There were three things that God was doing here, according to the information that we derive from inspiration:

God desired to:

- "prove the loyalty of His servant before all heaven,
- "demonstrate that nothing less than perfect obedience can be accepted,
- "open more fully before them the plan of salvation" (White, *Patriarchs and Prophets*, p. 154).

What do you think?

From: WP
To: Kevin Straub
Subject: Re: Abraham and Isaac
WP:
Thank you for this thoughtful response. I just reread the chapter you alluded to, and it certainly does counter my contentions. It is so hard for me to conceive that God would even hint at such an awful command which is so contrary to His character. It would seem so much more believable that He would do all the intervening (perhaps even placing the cloud over the mountain because He knew that was where the ram was …), and then one could apply Romans 8:28 to the bad situation that Satan had set up originally. Does something like this ever make you wonder whether some accounts written by EGW may have been less inspired than others? I

am not trying to create heresy. I know that she thought that God kills, and I wonder if that belief could ever skew her interpretation of events. Was this account shown to her in inspiration or was she reiterating the accepted thoughts of her day? I am really laying my soul bare by saying these things. I am not trying to be argumentative, but I struggle with these questions. Have you ever wondered about these things? Thanks for communicating with me. I would really appreciate your thoughts on this.

Kevin Straub:
Well, I think it is going far out on a limb to make these sorts of assumptions regarding the inspired page. *There is far too much filling in of detail in her account for it to be merely based upon a learned paradigm of understanding—*and a faulty one, at that. The Conflict of the Ages series was written based on a major vision, the details of which she could not remember, but that were recalled and filled in when it came time to write. Therefore, it either accurately portrays the story or it does not. If there are such holes in it, requiring uninspired filling, then it is not worth anything to us. We would be endlessly quibbling about what is reliable and what is human opinion. This sort of unreliability would prevent me from using the writings at all.

I cannot say that "she thought that God kills." I do not see this in the broad view of her writing. She herself stated that she would use Bible language and, if we have a problem with this, we must take it up with the Bible. There are so many clear statements—key statements—that outline the principles by which God destroys, that we can quite readily take these, in the same way as we do with biblical statements and use them to interpret the language. In those key statements, we *never* have any exception clauses written in. As an example, regarding angels:

> Angels are sent from the heavenly courts, not to destroy, but to watch over and guard imperiled souls, to save the lost, to bring the straying ones back to the fold. "I came not to condemn, but to save," Christ declared. (*The Review and Herald*, May 10, 1906, par. 15)

Note that such a statement *is never given* with a "back door" to allow for proactive violence, as *might* be written thus:

> Angels are sent from the heavenly courts, not to destroy, but to watch over and guard imperiled souls, to save the lost, to bring the straying ones back to the fold. "I came not to condemn, but to save," Christ declared. [*But those who will not be saved, He must destroy and He will employ the angels to do this work*] (with added italicized words not in original).

You never see such examples of "but" statements or exceptions given.

We could toy with the same questions and doubts with regard to the Bible. There are many cases in which God gives commands that are against His command, even regarding killing, in the eye-for-eye civil code and in the conduct of Israel in their use of the sword to vanquish their enemies. While these are based on God's accommodations to fallen humanity by giving guidance in the context of humanity's own chosen methods, there is the principle in operation here, it would seem, that *God can give a command that is contrary to His chosen way of doing things and that, under ordinary circumstances would, in fact, be out of character and which He would never give, and yet we would be in error were we to consider it an unrighteous command*.

When God came to Abraham saying that He was going to destroy Sodom, what do you think Abraham believed about that? I think he believed that God was going to destroy Sodom by using direct power to destroy. He then proceeded to negotiate with God based on a faulty understanding. Was God doing the same with Abraham, continuing in a charade, based upon a belief in something that He would never do? In other words, was God letting Abraham think He was negotiating down the terms by which He would refrain from exercising His power to destroy, when the part about Him destroying was not understood at all? God was not here addressing His methodologies. Instead, He was working within the context of the times, the culture, and the way of thinking and perceiving.

So, could it be a similar type of thing taking place, in which God's instruction to "Offer Isaac for a burnt offering," was letting Abraham think that He would allow him go through with such a command when there was no intent on His part to require or allow him to physically go through with it; instead, was an exercise to give a lesson to Abraham while at the same time testing his faith? These are acted parables, are they not? Consider these other examples of parabolic instructions, teachings, and enactments: "Rise, Peter, kill, and eat" (Acts 10:13); the rich man and Lazarus (Luke 16:19–22); and the angel posturing before Moses as though he would kill him (Exod. 4:24) are all examples of God using imagery and language that is not in harmony with the reality of His character and law. **[End of discussion with WP]**

Another Bible student asks:
How do you harmonize James 1:13 with the story of Abraham, particularly where it says "that God did tempt Abraham" in Genesis 22:1?

> Let no man say when he is tempted, I am tempted of God: for God cannot be tempted with evil, neither tempteth he any man: But every man is tempted, when he is drawn away of his own lust, and enticed. (James 1:13–14)

Kevin: All that we read of the Abraham/Isaac account in *Patriarchs and Prophets* and in the Bible is literally true and, at the same time, harmonizes perfectly with James' statement. Here is how that works:

In the Bible, you have two sets of statements or two manners of expression. One we call the "major voice" and the other the "minor voice." The major voice is that which is the standard cultural and idiomatic manner of Hebraic thought and expression, which is the "God-did-it" language. Ellen White calls it a "maxim."

> It was a maxim among the Jews that a failure to do good, when one had opportunity, was to do evil; to neglect to save life was to kill. (White, *The Desire of Ages*, p. 286)

Along with this, there was also confusion in the minds of the ancients regarding the character of God, as the concept of the destroyer, the rebel Lucifer, was not yet well developed in their theology and thinking. They generally believed that all things, good and evil, came from the one source. This pattern of thought would have been modelled upon the surrounding pagan nations' own concepts of deity.

Having said that, we do have the "minor voice," and God made sure to establish it early on, for to Moses He said that His anger was the hiding of His face and He explained how it was to work (see Deut. 31:16–18). In fact, it was so important as an interpretive key that God instructed Moses to make it into a song, so the people would not forget it.

Now, when we come to the Abrahamic story, we find that God tempted Abraham. Was Abraham tempted? Yes. Who tempted him? The Old Testament says that God did it. How? *By allowing Satan to tempt him*. Why? Because he had in himself character defects and issues of trusting God that needed to be overcome and which predisposed him to fall to this particular temptation. It is how "God" tempts all of us. James 1:14–15 explains it as being drawn away of *our own desires*. God allows us to meet with tests in order that we might recognize our propensities and weaknesses, so we would learn to lean harder on Him and overcome. Abraham had some serious trust issues, with a predisposition to take matters into his own hands. Two previous times, Abraham did things his own way, by producing a son of his own, when God said He would provide a son, and by protecting himself and Sarai and lying about their relationship.

> God had called Abraham to be the father of the faithful, and his life was to stand as an example of faith to succeeding generations. But his faith had not been perfect. He had shown distrust of God in concealing the fact that Sarah was his wife, and again in his marriage with Hagar. That he might reach the highest standard, God subjected him to another test, the closest which man was ever called to endure. In a vision of the night he was directed to repair to the land of Moriah, and there offer up his

son as a burnt offering upon a mountain that should be shown him. (White, *Patriarchs and Prophets*, p. 147)

God was at work here to break Abraham of his trust issues, so that he could truly become the father of the faithful. If he had refused to go through with the command of God, he would have failed. But he did not fail. He struggled along the way but at last, realizing that it was God Who spoke to him, he determined to obey.

> Satan was at hand to suggest that he must be deceived, for the divine law commands, "Thou shalt not kill," and God would not require what He had once forbidden. (White, *Patriarchs and Prophets*, p. 148)

> Satan was near to whisper doubts and unbelief, but Abraham resisted his suggestions. As they were about to begin the journey of the third day, the patriarch, looking northward, saw the promised sign, a cloud of glory hovering over Mount Moriah, and he knew that the voice which had spoken to him was from heaven. (White, *Patriarchs and Prophets*, p. 151)

> But Abraham does not reason; he obeys. His only hope is that the God who can do all things will raise his son from the dead. The knife was raised, but it did not fall. God spoke, "It is enough." The faith of the father and the submission of the son were fully tested. "… For now I know that thou fearest God, seeing thou hast not withheld thy son, thine only son from me." (White, *Patriarchs and Prophets*, p. 152)

> Abraham's test was the most severe that could ever come to a human being. Had he then turned from God, he would never have been registered as the father of the faithful. Had he deviated from God's command, the world would have lost this rich example of faith in God and victory over unbelief. (White, *Christ Triumphant*, p. 83)

So, God allows Satan to come to Abraham and tempt him. Satan did not come telling Abraham to offer Isaac as a sacrifice; rather, he tortured him with the thought that surely God would not require this of him. We find this a type of how Satan came to Christ. How did Satan tempt Christ? From beginning to end, it was to tempt Him to doubt the voice of God and doubt His mission as the sacrificial Lamb. In the wilderness temptation (as described in Matthew 4:1–4), and at the outset of His ministry, Satan was there offering Him earthly rulership over all the kingdoms of the world (Matt. 4:8–10)—not through sacrifice but through compromise and taking matters into His own hands. At the end, he enjoined Christ to "save yourself. If you are the Son of God, come down from the cross" (Matt. 27:40). In between, Satan worked even through the disciples to pressure Jesus to take up an earthly kingdom of glory and shun the path of the cross. Peter said concerning Him suffering at Jerusalem and being killed "Be it far from thee, Lord" (Matt. 16:22), to which Christ gave a direct rebuke, bypassing Peter and speaking to Satan: "Get thee behind me, Satan …." (Matt. 16:23). But it was, in fact, God's purpose to "send" Him to the cross. "It pleased the Lord to bruise Him," and to "make His soul an offering for sin" (Isa. 53:9–10). This is "major voice" language.

Satan did not come telling Abraham to offer Isaac as a sacrifice; rather, he tortured him with the thought that surely God would not require this of him.

In trying to protect the "character of God" teaching, many have "overshot" the mark on this story and missed its real significance, failing to carefully question *the true nature of the temptation*! Where the confusion comes in, in this story, is not that God allowed a temptation to come to Abraham, but what that temptation was. Was the temptation for Abraham to offer up Isaac? No! Abraham was *not* tempted to offer up Isaac! Abraham did not want to do this, by any means! The temptation was to *not* offer Isaac. Satan desired that Abraham would doubt that it was the voice of God and fail to go through with the command. This is where Satan came to

Abraham, in the same way as when he came to Christ! If Abraham had been tempted by Satan to offer Isaac and had gone through with it (God had to stop him) *then Abraham would have failed that test*, right?

Coming back to that chapter in James, we find the clear statement that God does not tempt. To harmonize this, we must realize again that there are two voices, or two usages, in language. James is not speaking in the "major voice," but is speaking the straight language of "minor voice."

Does God kill? Yes. The Bible says so:

> I kill, and I make alive. (Deut. 32:39)

Does God kill? No. The Bible says so:

> The thief cometh not, but for to steal, and to kill, and to destroy:
> I am come that they might have life, and that they might have [it]
> more abundantly. (John 10:10)

And we could go on through many such illustrations from the Scriptures. Two voices. The major voice of Bible language must be interpreted to harmonize with the minor voice of insight as written into the narrative and interpretive keys given in the Scriptures, not the other way around. In fact, you cannot reverse it. It would be total confusion. For Christ came to show the character of God, and we see the minor voice of Scripture revealed in Him, although He is *physically* the Major Voice! (See Matthew 17:3–5, showing us that the disciples revered the minor voices of Moses and Elijah, but God pointed to the Major Voice of God in the flesh: "hear ye *him*," [emphasis added]). The major voice in Scripture—in language—is idiomatic. God "tempts" by allowing trials and tests to come and not arbitrarily, either—they come because of sin. They come because of choices that have been made in the past, which have damaged our relationship with God and which can only be repaired through testing and trial.

CHAPTER 10

Jesus Invades Jericho, Demolishes Walls, Thousands Killed

> *"The Christian soldier is the man who never fights with carnal weapons, and whose only sword is 'the sword of the Spirit,' which is the word of God."*
> E.J. Waggoner, "A Wise Answer," *The Present Truth* [UK], Apr. 19, 1894, p. 256.9

Jericho, in filling up the cup of its iniquity, fell under the judgment of God. As He instructed the utter decimation of its inhabitants, the atheist has found fertile ground for making accusations of despotism against Him.

> Indeed, this whole question of judgment upon the wicked reveals the inconsistency in the attitude of the skeptic. How often a scoffer hurls at Christians the inquiry, "If there is a God in heaven who rules and directs affairs, why does He permit evil men to dominate this world and to carry on all their terrible practices that bring sorrow and trouble to poor innocent creatures?" Then the same scoffer will turn around a little later

and ask sneeringly, "If God is a God of love, as you Christians declare, why did He bring destruction on people at different times in the world, and why is He finally going to destroy all except a select group?" But the skeptic does not seem to realize that the first question finds its answer in the second. And accordingly, he does not realize that he is inconsistent in raising a clamor against the judgments of God when he has just inquired why God does not wreak vengeance upon evildoers. (White, *The Seventh-day Adventist Bible Commentary*, Vol. 2, p. 202)

The problem before us in connection with the destruction of the Canaanites by the Israelites, then, is simply this: first, to prove that the Canaanites were rebels against God's government, thus to demonstrate the justice of God in having them destroyed; second, to prove that they had been given a period of grace and probation, thus to demonstrate the mercy and long-suffering of God. It is not difficult to prove both of these propositions.

As to the first, it is a simple matter of history that the peoples on the eastern seaboard of the Mediterranean were as corrupt and depraved as any who have ever dwelt upon this earth. They made a religion of lust. They sent their children into the fires of the god Molech. Lev. 18 presents briefly something of the moral rebellion of the Canaanites. The imagination and a little knowledge of history supply the rest. According to the Bible, the Canaanites were so vile that the very land "spued" them out (Lev. 18:28) ....

As to the second proposition, the Bible is equally explicit. In the 15th chapter of Genesis is the record of the promise of God to Abraham, that his seed should inherit the land of Canaan. The explanation that God gave to Abraham as to why the promise would be so long in fulfilling, was that "the iniquity of the Amorites is not yet full" (v. 16). The Amorites here stand for the peoples of Canaan, for they were the powerful, dominant race.

There is no statement anywhere in the OT that more clearly sets forth the fact of God's mercy to sinners, and of how He gives to them a time of probation. (*The Seventh-day Adventist Bible Commentary*, Vol. 2, p. 200)

Here was Abraham, the friend of God. The Lord desired to give to him the land of Canaan for an inheritance. If God had been like an earthly ruler, He would doubtless have taken immediate steps to see that His promise was fulfilled for His favorite, and would have driven out or put to the sword all who stood in the way. That has been the history of despots who had all power in their hands. But not so with God. He declared in effect to Abraham, You must be patient. Your children and your children's children to the fourth generation must also be patient. My love to you is great. I long to fulfill for you and yours My promise. Nothing would bring greater pleasure to My heart. But—ah, here is the significant fact. Did the Lord say But I have no power to fulfill My promise now? No; He had all power. He could have sent fire from heaven suddenly to consume all the inhabitants of Canaan. No, that was not the problem. The delay was because the cup of the "iniquity of the Amorites is not yet full." In other words, they had not completely sinned away their day of grace. There was still further mercy to be extended to them. God's Spirit was yet to plead with their hearts.

And so for 400 years more, generation after generation of the Amorites was permitted to live and to practice increasing abominations. Then God ordered their destruction. The reasonable conclusion is that their destruction was decreed because their cup of iniquity was full, that nothing would be gained by further extending mercy to them. (White, *The Seventh-day Adventist Bible Commentary*, Vol. 2, pp. 200–201)

We should ever keep in mind that God's mercy endures forever. Yet it cannot be extended any further than the consent of the free moral agent.

When all righteousness is so utterly repudiated, Satan lies in wait to urge his right to impose his will upon them, and God cannot do anything but give them over to his valid claim, for they have chosen. This is the principle of Divine judgment. In this story, and many others, judgment was executed through His own people, in their use of the sword. This adds a dimension that makes it difficult to see God's character, for it appears that He is merely destroying at arm's length, using His people to do His dirty work. This has been covered previously, as we have discovered that it was the will of His people to take up arms. God did not force them to rely upon His own methods but gave them over to their decision. His instructions to them were in keeping with *their* decision, not *His*.

E. J. Waggoner wrote some amazing things about God's character and government relating to the idea of conquest by force of arms. The sword of steel was never to be in the mind of God's people, not in conquest nor "even in self-defense" for we are to trust in God as our Provider and Defender ("The Everlasting Covenant," p. 127). "It will be seen that there is nothing like force in the government of God, nothing like compulsion. If there were, his reign would not be a reign of peace. It is altogether different from any earthly government that exists, or that ever did exist" (E.J. Waggoner, "The Reign of Peace," *The Signs of the Times,* Vol. 19, Oct. 9, 1893, p. 706.32).

Waggoner explains why the Israelites fought:

> But the children of Israel did fight throughout all their natural existence, and under God's direction, too, it will be urged. That is very true, but it does not at all prove that it was God's purpose that they should fight. We must not forget that 'their minds were blinded' by unbelief, so that they could not perceive the purpose of God for them. They did not grasp the spiritual realities of the kingdom of God, but were content with shadows instead; and the same God who bore with their hardness of heart in the beginning, and strove to teach them by shadows, when they would not have the substance, still remained with

them, compassionately considerate of their infirmities. God himself suffered them, because of the hardness of their hearts, to have a plurality of wives, and even laid down rules regulating polygamy, in order to diminish as far as possible the resulting evils, but that does not prove that He designed it for them. We well know that "from the beginning it was not so." So when Jesus forbade His followers to fight in any cause whatever, He introduced nothing new, any more than when He taught that a man should have but one wife, and should cleave to her as long as he lived. He was simply enunciating first principles—preaching a thorough reformation. (Waggoner, "Why the Israelites Fought," *The Everlasting Covenant*, p. 385)

Yet one more thing must be remembered in connection with this question of fighting and the possession of the land of Canaan, the promised inheritance, and that is that the children of Israel did not get it after all, with all their fighting. The same promise that was given them, remains for us; "but if Joshua had given them rest, then would He not afterwards have spoken of another day" in which to seek and find it. The reason why they did not get it, was their unbelief, and that was why they fought. If they had believed the Lord, they would have allowed Him to clear the land of its totally depraved inhabitants, in the way that He proposed. They in the meantime would not have been idle, but would have performed the work of faith which God set them. (Waggoner, "War Not a Success," *The Everlasting Covenant*, p. 387)

The Scriptures tell us that it was, in fact, *by faith*, that the walls of Jericho fell (Heb. 11:30). It is true that, after the walls fell, the Israelites went in and slaughtered all living creatures, human and animal, per God's directions. They still had the sword in their hands and, under permissive will, they had to follow His counsel to make the work as complete as if it would have been done by God's ways (Straub, *Awesome God: Songs of His*

Power, Volume 1, Chapter 5). But the walls did not fall by the Israelites' sword, nor any other instrument of physical battle. Those walls fell by other forces. God instructed them to march around the city every day for a week and to use their trumpets—hardly a viable method of warfare, by human standards.

> In obedience to the divine command Joshua marshaled the armies of Israel. No assault was to be made. They were simply to make the circuit of the city, bearing the ark of God and blowing upon trumpets. First came the warriors, a body of chosen men, not now to conquer by their own skill and prowess, but by obedience to the directions given them from God …. **No sound was heard but the tread of that mighty host and the solemn peal of the trumpets**, echoing among the hills and resounding through the streets of Jericho. The circuit completed, the army returned in silence to their tents, and the ark was restored to its place in the tabernacle. (White, *Patriarchs and Prophets*, p. 488, emphasis added)

Do we have any direct statement to reveal what forces were exerted upon the structure of the walls that they would have fallen in such a remarkable manner? We have reference to the sight and sound of the marching host of Israel, each under the standard of their own tribe, as they bore the ark around the city each day for seven days. "All was silent, save *the* **measured tread** of many feet, and the occasional sound of the trumpet, breaking the stillness of the early morning" (White, *Patriarchs and Prophets*, p. 491, emphasis added).

Some think that Christ and His angels went directly at the walls with their own power because of the typical language used in relation to God's actions in punishing His enemies and delivering His people.

> God intended to show the Israelites that the conquest of Canaan was not to be ascribed to them. The captain of the Lord's host overcame Jericho. He and his angels were engaged in the

conquest. Christ commanded the armies of Heaven to throw down the walls of Jericho, and prepare an entrance for Joshua and the armies of Israel. God, in this wonderful miracle, not only strengthened the faith of his people in his power to subdue their enemies, but rebuked their former unbelief. (White, *The Spirit of Prophecy*, Vol. 1, p. 351)

Remember that Christ and His angels bring about a condition conducive to destruction when they *withdraw*, according to the "hiding of face" principle (Ibid., Chapter 7). God removes His hedge of protection, and then Satan can go to work with greater latitude, which he often does, while pointing to God as the one doing that work. But not always would we find direct Satanic activity. It can be that the forces of human activity are permitted to run their course, or the forces of nature are let loose to act with chaotic results. The first thing one might suspect in this story is that the pounding, rhythmic footfalls of the marching Israelites worked in such a way as to soften the walls at weak points, with trumpet blasts also working to the same end through the effect of harmonic resonance. Then, on the last day, in conjunction with a mighty sonic assault, there was an earthquake. Did it cause the earthquake?

> *Then, on the last day, in conjunction with a mighty sonic assault, there was an earthquake. Did it cause the earthquake?*

> The massive walls of solid stone seemed to defy the siege of men. The watchers on the walls looked on **with rising fear**, as, the first circuit ended, there followed a second, then a third, a fourth, a fifth, a sixth. What could be the object of these mysterious movements? What mighty event was impending? They had not long to wait. As the seventh circuit was completed, the long procession paused, **The trumpets, which for an interval**

> had been silent, now broke forth in a blast that shook the very earth. The walls of solid stone, with their massive towers and battlements, tottered and heaved from their foundations, and with a crash fell in ruin to the earth. The inhabitants of Jericho were **paralyzed with terror**, and the hosts of Israel marched in and took possession of the city. (White, *Patriarchs and Prophets*, p. 491, emphasis added)

Whether the trumpets *caused* or merely *coincided* with an earthquake, we do not know for certain. We see that the Spirit of Prophecy says that the trumpet blast shook the earth. Is that a literary thing, or literal? But it does not matter. If it was an earthquake, it would be a straightforward effect of God withdrawing His protective hand from the elements. If the marches and the trumpets were the agency of force, God was fulfilling His promise by having the Israelites perform an action calculated to open the way into the city so that they could easily take it under permissive will, with no resistance being made as the inhabitants were not prepared to fight, being "paralyzed with terror" (White, *Patriarchs and Prophets*, p. 491.1). We could very well view this story as a mixture of God using the fear principle of "the hornet," which we shall discuss shortly, in conjunction with the paradigm of permissive will.

> And it came to pass, when all the kings of the Amorites, which [were] on the side of Jordan westward, and all the kings of the Canaanites, which [were] by the sea, heard that the LORD had dried up the waters of Jordan from before the children of Israel, until we were passed over, that **their heart melted, neither was there spirit in them any more, because of the children of Israel** (Josh. 5:1, emphasis added).

> In some instances the report of God's mighty deeds on behalf of His people would have **smitten the Canaanites with fear** and they would have surrendered without out fighting (Num. 22:3;

Joshua 2:9–11; Deut. 28:10; Ex. 23:27; Deut. 2:25; 11:25; Ex. 15:13–16; Joshua 5:1; Ex. 34:24; cf. Gen. 35:5; Joshua 10:1, 2; 1 Sam. 14:15; 2 Chron. 17:10). At other times they would have **become confused**, and turned on one another (Judges 7:22; 1 Sam. 14:20; 2 Chron. 20:20–24). Also, God would have utilized, at times, the **forces of nature** (Joshua 10:11, 12; etc.) even as He had done in Egypt, at the Red Sea, and at the crossing of the Jordan. Had Israel only cooperated with Him, He would have worked for them in many unexpected ways. Perhaps, too, some nations—like the Gibeonites (PP 507, 508)—would have come to a knowledge of the true God.

But Israel's repeated failure to give strict obedience to God's commands at Kadesh (PP 394), Shittim (Num. 25:1–9), and Ai (Joshua 7:8, 9; PP 494) **in large measure allayed the fears of the Canaanites, gave them time to prepare for the fray, and made the conquest of the land far more difficult than it would otherwise have been** (PP 437). Nevertheless, divine love no longer availing to bring repentance, divine justice decreed the probation of these rebels against God closed, demanded their prompt execution, and assigned their land to His chosen representatives (see Num. 23:19–24; PP 492; cf. GC 37; Matt. 21:41, 43). (*Seventh-day Adventist Bible Commentary*, Vol. 2, pp. 203–204, emphasis added)

Elder Waggoner writes:

Just as the Lord did to Pharoah and to all Egypt, so did he promise to do to all the enemies that should set themselves against the progress of the Israelites to the promised land. But the children of Israel did not strike a single blow to effect their deliverance from Egypt and the overthrow of all its armies. When Moses, forty years before, had attempted to deliver Israel by physical force, he most signally failed, and was obliged to flee in disgrace. It was only when he knew the Gospel as the power of God unto salvation, that he was able to lead the people forth without any fear of the wrath of the king. This is conclusive proof that God did not design that they should fight for the possession of the land; and if they did not fight, of course they could not lose any of their number in battle. Read further as to the manner in which God proposed to give them the land. (Waggoner, *The Everlasting Covenant*, p. 383.2)

To conclude this study, we circle back to "the hornet," as Waggoner next cites Exodus 23:27–30, and look into the "hornet principle."

Hornets are nasty things. They will oftentimes attack entirely unprovoked, with a painful sting, sometimes even fatally, depending on the species or the level of tolerance of the panicked recipient. But whether you are allergic to hornets or not, what is your reaction to a hornet on the offensive? Does fear make you flail about in a frenzy? Would you not appear to temporarily lose your mind as you flee to safety?

In the Bible, God tells the Israelites that He would "send the hornet" to drive out the enemies from the land which would then be available for the Israelites to move in and claim.

> I will **send my fear before thee**, and will destroy all the people to whom thou shalt come, and I will make all thine enemies turn their backs unto thee. And **I will send hornets before thee**, which shall drive out the Hivite, the Canaanite, and the Hittite, from before thee. (Exodus 23:27–30, emphasis added)

Note the parallelism in these verses, which is evidence that the hornets are a symbol for fear.

> Moreover the LORD thy God will **send the hornet among them**, until they that are left, and hide themselves from thee, be destroyed. (Deuteronomy 7:20, emphasis added)

> And **I sent the hornet before you**, which drave them out from before you, even the two kings of the Amorites; but not with thy sword, nor with thy bow. (Joshua 24:12, emphasis added)

What does it mean, *send the hornet*? Is it literal? Was the Lord going to dispossess the enemies of His people by bringing a plague of stinging insects? I believe that while this could be one possibility in keeping with the general idea of pestilential plagues, it would not be the primary intent of the use of *hornet* in this context. I believe that *the hornet* is symbolic of something different; that we might call it a "psychological operation" (PSYOP).

Note how in Joshua 24:12 that the two kings of the Amorites would be driven out by *the hornet* and not by the force of arms in the hands of the Israelites. How can it say this? We have the record of history that says that the Israelites warred against them successfully:

> And Israel smote him with the edge of the sword, and possessed his land from Arnon unto Jabbok, even unto the children of Ammon: for the border of the children of Ammon was strong .... So they smote him, and his sons, and all his people, until there was none left him alive: and they possessed his land. (Numbers 21:24, 35)

So, then, what does it mean, "but not with thy sword, nor with thy bow" (Josh. 24:12)? I cite the *Seventh-day Adventist Bible Commentary* on this point, with comment following:

> It seems clear that the signal victory over these kings was not due to the skill of the sword and bow, but rather to the special blessing of God. **Hornets, then, seem to be figurative of the assistance God provided to give success to the armies of Israel**. The figure is appropriate. As hornets would produce consternation and panic in a camp, so the Lord would send fear, terror, quaking, and confusion into the camp of the nations to unnerve them for battle. (Vol. 2, p. 296)

The *Commentary* agrees that hornets are a figure or symbol. While it speaks of the assistance that God provided to His own, it reveals His method—how He "sent" (allowed) confusion into the enemy camp to "unnerve them for battle." How this is done is by *recession*—He "hides His face." God can no longer keep them to the same degree as before; His angels are called away and His Spirit can no longer influence minds. Then they are subject to any number of problems, often psychological, as in **"I will send my fear before thee"** (Exod. 23:27, emphasis added). When this happens, they are reduced to a greatly weakened state in which they become ripe for defeat.

The words of Rahab, when hiding the spies Joshua and Caleb, demonstrated this principle when she recounted to them her people's present state of mind. Her people knew the story of the Exodus and, although it was marred by the rebellion of the Israelites forty years earlier, the second approach was viewed with consternation because of the recent victories God had given His people once again:

> And she said unto the men, I know that the LORD hath given you the land, and that **your terror is fallen upon us**, and that **all the inhabitants of the land faint because of you**. For we have heard how the LORD dried up the water of the Red sea for you, when ye came out of Egypt; and what ye did unto the two kings of the Amorites, that were on the other side Jordan, Sihon and Og, whom ye utterly destroyed. And as soon as we had heard these things, **our hearts did melt, neither did there remain any more courage in any man**, because of you: for the LORD your God, he [is] God in heaven above, and in earth beneath. (Joshua 2:9–11, emphasis added)

Inspiration explains how God would have worked for the success of His people, how He would have fought.

> God had promised His people that if they would obey His voice He would go before them and fight for them; and **He would also send hornets to drive out the inhabitants of the land.** (White, *Patriarchs and Prophets*, p. 436, emphasis added)

However, a generation earlier, when the people rebelled and were sent back to the wilderness to perish, they immediately rebelled a second time and went in against God's approval, to war without His help. They were cut down badly in the process, and this defeat gave occasion for the inhabitants of the land to discount the power attending their way. God became to them as a false god and any previous reports to the contrary were considered as lore, "fake news," to put in today's terms. Thus, "the fears of the nations had not been generally aroused" (White, *Patriarchs and Prophets*, p. 436). Now, as the Israelites went on the move once again toward the border, they had to fight a much harder battle than they would have had before.

> **The fears of the nations had not been generally aroused**, and little preparation had been made to oppose their progress. But when the Lord now bade Israel go forward, they must advance against alert and powerful foes, and must contend with large and well-trained armies that had been preparing to resist their approach. (White, *Patriarchs and Prophets*, p. 436, emphasis added)

There we can see that "the hornet" that God would send alludes to the arousal of a spirit of fear in the enemy nations. Again, this is *language*. God does not give a spirit of fear, but of **"a sound mind"** (2 Tim. 1:7). This "arousal" of fear means that they would be given over to it by the withdrawal of His Spirit of love and power and straight thinking.

> For if ye shall diligently keep all these commandments which I command you, to do them, to love the LORD your God, to walk in all his ways, and to cleave unto him; Then will **the LORD drive out all these nations** from before you, and ye shall possess greater nations and mightier than yourselves .... There shall no man be able to stand before you: for **the LORD your God shall lay the fear of you and the dread of you upon all the land that ye shall tread upon**, as he hath said unto you. (Deuteronomy 11:22–25, emphasis added)

I believe the primary meaning of the symbol of the hornet to be the state of fear arousal that would cause the enemy to flee before or at their advance, or to fortify for a fight, in which case God would manifest His signal power to cause them to fall to His people through the blessing of protection upon His own and not upon the others, often manifest as a confusion causing the enemy to destroy themselves.

There is another valid etiological outcome of the symbol of the pestilential insect, as a figure of *the use of nations to punish other nations*. God refers to this principle of operation, in which the interplay of national powers arrayed against each other is spoken of as *His doing*. Of course, this is not the case physically, that is, as God does not give command to idolatrous forces, for them to obey willingly or otherwise. Rather, it is the play of the course of events which He foresees and allows. As we would see a nation becoming more disconnected from righteousness, crossing that line where God can no longer extend mercy and exert power to save it, it becomes prey to other nations that are yet higher up on the protection scale.

It is interesting that the very next line in *The Seventh-day Adventist Bible Commentary* passage states, "Some see in these hornets the Egyptians whom the Lord used to weaken Canaanitish nations so as to make them as easy prey to the Israelites" (White, *The Seventh-day Adventist Bible Commentary*, Vol. 2, p. 296). In Isaiah, He refers to other nations as pestilential insects. "And it shall come to pass in that day, that **the LORD shall hiss for the fly** that is in the uttermost part of the rivers of Egypt, **and for the bee** that is in the land of Assyria" (Isa. 7:18, emphasis added).

Back to the *Commentary* again, we see that this would refer to the nations, not to the literal insects:

> 18. **Hiss for the fly**. Literally, "whistle to the fly" to come from the distant parts of Egypt, that is, **summon the armies of Egypt** ....
>
> **The bee**. Assyria is compared to a bee. Bees here symbolize a persistent and formidable enemy (Deut. 1:44; Ps. 118:12). The sting of a bee, however painful, is seldom fatal. Assyria would come against Judah as the rod of God's anger (Isa. 10:5–7), but the nation would not perish.
>
> 19. **They shall come**. The figure of invading insects is continued. The Egyptians and Assyrians would come into the land like flies

and bees, and would penetrate all parts of the country. (White, *The Seventh-day Adventist Bible Commentary*, Vol. 4, p. 137)

In conclusion, learn how to actively apply these interpretive tools when you read about God sending the hornet or other insects to drive out the enemy. He is not a sadist or a torturer, yet He will allow the consequences of godlessness to come to pass, whether it is an infestation of real pests, such as we saw in the Egyptian plagues; or the terror and confusion of a fear-induced psychosis; or aggressor nations coming down upon morally fallen nations given up to the burden of their own wickedness. We must take time to grapple with all these concepts as exemplified in the Bible, comparing scripture with scripture and with history. By understanding the goodness of God and that His methods of warfare are not like that of carnal humanity, we will rightly divide the scriptures at last. We are thankful for God's great blessing that He bestows as we grapple with the language in the careful reading of His Word.

CHAPTER 11

Vengeance Is the Lord's: The Samson Debacle—Homicidal Maniac or Icon of Faith?

> *"And the times of this ignorance God winked at; but now commandeth all men every where to repent: Because he hath appointed a day, in the which he will judge the world in righteousness."*
> Acts 17:30–31

The story of Samson is one of debauchery, which is defined as "indulgence in sensual pleasures; excessive or immoral activities involving sex, food, or intoxicants" The life story of this man is undeniably a debacle, the definition of which is "a disastrous or embarrassing failure" (WordWeb 10.23 Copyright Antony Lewis 2022).

Samson had transgressed the command of God by taking a wife from the Philistines, and again he ventured among them—now his deadly enemies—in the indulgence of unlawful passion. Trusting to his great strength, which had inspired the Philistines with such terror, he went boldly to Gaza, to visit a harlot of that place …. The accusing voice of conscience filled him with remorse, as he remembered that he had broken his vow as a Nazarite. (White, *Patriarchs and Prophets*, p. 564)

He continued to seek those sensuous pleasures that were luring him to ruin. "He loved a woman in the valley of Sorek," not far from his own birthplace. Her name was Delilah, "the consumer." The vale of Sorek was celebrated for its vineyards; these also had a temptation for the wavering Nazarite, who had already indulged in the use of wine, thus breaking another tie that bound him to purity and to God. (White, *Patriarchs and Prophets*, p. 565)

God's promise that through Samson He would "begin to deliver Israel out of the hand of the Philistines" was fulfilled; but how dark and terrible the record of that life which might have been a praise to God and a glory to the nation! **Had Samson been true to his divine calling, the purpose of God could have been accomplished in his honor and exaltation.** But he yielded to temptation and proved untrue to his trust, and **his mission was fulfilled in defeat, bondage, and death.** (White, *Patriarchs and Prophets*, p. 567, emphasis added)

God's promise was fulfilled, but it was messy, and done under "permissive paradigm," wherein Satan was able to function under the guise of the Spirit of God. The examination we shall make of this story will challenge the long-held belief that it was by the direct aid of God that Samson performed his mighty exploits.

I believe that in the Samson narrative, Satan has gained much traction in his promotion of the lie portraying a capricious and vengeful God. Now, as we are growing up into the Lord, we must no longer be as children, buffeted about by the superstitious and dark views of God. We must approach this story as principle-based, as well. The facts that shape my thinking on this story are as follows:

1. Samson had strength beyond what could have been generated by human muscle, attached to bone and sinew. In other words, the stresses put upon the human frame by the physical actions taken by Samson are beyond what could be

endured without doing bodily damage. Examining cases of drug-induced, super-human strength, we find that muscles can be exerted to such an extent that damage is done to connection points where they attach to the skeletal structure, even to the breaking of the bones themselves. Another example of this would be in cases of electrocution, where the contractions of muscles can be so strong that they will damage one's own body. It is my conclusion that there had to have been supernatural assistance by angels in at least *some* of the recorded episodes.

2. God's angels do not destroy and kill.
3. The principle by which we interpret God's involvement in destruction and death as the "wrath of God," is that God honors freedom of choice by "giving over" in four distinct areas, which can bear upon a situation *alone* or *in combination*: a) wicked self; b) wicked others (humans); c) wicked angels; or d) nature gone to chaos.
4. How did God "give over" in the case of Samson? This is where we must focus our study. There are layers of Divine wrath, or "giving over," in this story. God must have "given over" Samson in his personal thinking, just as Israel in general was "given over" to believe that it must operate by the sword to conquer its enemies and that violent conquest was a divinely approved method. Under this paradigm, as Samson gave himself over to wickedness, God gave him over to Satan. *Satan would then have operated as a "poser," making Samson, national Israel, the historical inspired writer of the narrative in Judges, as well as later inspired writers—and we the readers of those records—believe that God and His angels were involved in proactive destruction through Samson.*

In unraveling all of this, we have to work carefully to diligently apply the principles of God's government and character, seeing that we have fallen into the same error of thinking as had Israel—that God enjoined the use of the sword. As Ellen White has said, we have "many" lessons to *learn*, and "many, many" to *unlearn* (Testimonies to Ministers, p. 30.2). This is hard for minds steeped in traditional thinking, especially when they are not willing to lay aside all unnecessary pursuits to study and stretch the mind to the utmost to answer the difficult questions. The *foolish virgins,* she says, "have not studied His character" (White, *Christ's Object Lessons*, p. 411, para. 1).

The narrative of Samson is not an easy one to decipher according to the principles of God's character. In our teaching to others of the advanced light on the character of God, this story is best left until later, after many of the more easily interpreted stories have been studied and until there is a thorough understanding of the principles of God's wrath and the theology of permissive paradigm. The Samson narrative can be somewhat of a "test case," I believe, to show whether we are willing to come all the way out of unbiblical and dark views about God. This is because of the difficulties it presents; a) by its employment of pure "biblical language" wherein little or no breaks are given in either the Bible or the Spirit of Prophecy pages that we can point to as hard contextual evidence that God was not proactively involved in Samson's exploits; and b) because of Samson's inclusion in the "hall of faith" in Hebrews, Chapter 11.

Samson's prayer in Judges 16:28 is not a holy prayer. Samson wanted to kill for self-revenge. I do not believe this final act was done in God's power; first, because God does not perpetrate violence; and second, God does not take revenge by repaying evil with evil; third, all that is done is to be for the glory of God and Samson's motivation for killing all of those Philistines was clearly to have selfish revenge; and fourth, his last act was suicide. A mass murder-suicide. To believe that God's power was employed in answer to this prayer is to find in the story of Samson a rationale for religiously motivated terrorism.

Samson prays:

> And Samson called unto the LORD, and said, O Lord GOD, remember me, I pray thee, and strengthen me, I pray thee, only

this once, O God, that I may be at once **avenged of the Philistines for my two eyes.** (Judges 16:28, emphasis added)

The teaching of Jesus as applied to the case of Samson:

Ye have heard that it hath been said, **An eye for an eye**, and a tooth for a tooth: But **I say unto you, That ye resist not evil**: but whosoever shall smite thee on thy right cheek, turn to him the other also. (Matthew 5:38–39)

The teaching of Paul, who was taught directly of Jesus:

Recompense to no man evil for evil. Provide things honest in the sight of all men. If it be possible, as much as lieth in you, live peaceably with all men. Dearly beloved, avenge not yourselves, but rather give place unto wrath: for it is written, Vengeance is mine; I will repay, saith the Lord. Therefore if thine enemy hunger, feed him; if he thirst, give him drink: for in so doing thou shalt heap coals of fire on his head. Be not overcome of evil, but overcome evil with good. (Romans 12:17–21)

How does God treat His enemies?

Love worketh no ill to his neighbour: therefore love is the fulfilling of the law. (Romans 13:10)

Then said Jesus, Father, forgive them; for they know not what they do. (Luke 23:34)

But I say unto you, Love your enemies, bless them that curse you, do good to them that hate you, and pray for them which despitefully use you, and persecute you; That ye may be the children of your Father which is in heaven: for he maketh his sun to rise on the evil and on the good, and sendeth rain on the just and on the unjust. (Matthew 5:44–45)

Was God different in the Old Testament? "Jesus Christ the same yesterday, and to day, and for ever. Be not carried about with divers and strange doctrines" [such as God kills?] (Heb. 13:8–9).

Earlier in my understanding of the truth about God's character and methods, I shied away from the idea of Satanic involvement in Samson's feats, because it seemed to enter dangerous ground, such as the "Two Lords" principle that promotes the idea that Satan interposed as the Lord in the Old Testament, to such extremes that we are to believe that it was Satan giving the law at Mt. Sinai (Clute, *Into the Father's Heart*). Yet, as I continually found myself cornered on this story, I had to revisit this concept to see if there might not be some merit in it, at least in some instances such as the Samson story. So, I started looking at this concept from the point of view that the false paradigm of a destroying God *is*, in fact, Satanic. The notion that violence can and should be employed in righteousness to make one's way in the world or to teach the character of God is antithetical to the truth about the character of God and is the teaching of the enemy of all righteousness. We must fix in our mind the undeviating principle that "Jesus Christ is the Restorer. Satan, the apostate, is the destroyer. **Here** is the conflict between the Prince of life and the prince of this world, the power of darkness" (White, *Christ Triumphant*, p. 247, emphasis added). Samson was using violence in such a way as to be avenged for himself in a situation created by his own hedonistic lust for wanton living under the guise of being a man of God bringing deliverance to His people against the Philistine enemy. God's purposes were achieved in the destruction of the Philistines but God really didn't have anything to do with how it was done. God's purposes to reveal Himself were decidedly **not** achieved in the "ministry" of Samson as Nazarite, for Samson repudiated that role.

Therefore, Samson had to be operating as fully given over to the idea of a destructive God, as was his entire culture. His parents believed God kills, and this would have been taught to Samson (Judges 13:23, 24). This is not to say that if Samson had remained righteous in all his ways that God would have lent supernatural strength to him to be used in destructive ways. To the contrary, it would have been employed righteously and

> *God is the master of the "plan B" scenario. He has a thousand ways to patiently work out His purposes.*

would have vindicated the character of God. *It would have been, instead of a difficult and confusing story, a powerful lesson for all of us as to the truths about God that we are now uncovering*. At this time, however, we find that the narrative of Samson's experience has become more of a hindrance to God's purposes than a help, even though the inspired pen states:

> God's promise that through Samson He would "begin to deliver Israel out of the hand of the Philistines" was fulfilled. (White, *Patriarchs and Prophets*, p. 567)

Here is how—according to the "giving over" principle—that the deliverance came because God handed the Philistines over to the wickedness of Samson, with the usurper, Satan, acting in the background! It is not an isolated instance of God using evil actors to carry out his purposes, as in the Assyrian, whom God gave the dubious distinction of being the "rod of mine anger" (Isa. 10:5). It certainly wasn't the way God would have intended for His deliverance to be carried out, but God's purposes were fulfilled in spite of the evil of men and women.

Let me digress for a moment to comment on this.

God is the master of the "plan B" scenario. He has a thousand ways to patiently work out His purposes. The underlying principle is that His character and love find a way to turn evil around for good. This is the overarching principle that operates in the big picture of the great controversy, wherein God turns the whole experiment in rebellion on its head to fulfill His purpose to have many sons and daughters with Him on the throne. This is achieved through the redemption plan of sending Himself into the human experience to make the way for fusing the Divine nature with the human nature in an eternal bond. This is the grandest theme for our contemplation.

As Samson descended into sin and degradation, God, in justice, had to give him over so far to Satan that the latter could interpose to the degree that we have on record. This is nothing less than Divine wrath, and Samson was surely smitten with it (Isa. 57:17). These stories of killing and destruction took place because of Samson's lack of self-control and passion, and they have nothing to do with uplifting the God of heaven and bringing honor and glory to His name. It was not about God; it was all about Samson and his anger-management issues! In the manner typical of these personality disorders, Samson blamed others for his own problems and took it out by resorting to vandalism and murder. Unfortunately, at that time, the whole societal/cultural paradigm of understanding of Divine anger and deliverance functioned as a de facto *enabler* of Samson's actions. In this modality, under permissive will, Samson could freely act out as a petulant child without any sanction from his own culture.

As Samson was given over, evil angels were given license to act. The Egyptian plagues have also been attributed to the proactive hand of God, but the Scriptures say otherwise:

> He gave up their cattle also to the hail, and their flocks to hot thunderbolts.
>
> He cast upon them the fierceness of his anger, wrath, and indignation, and trouble, **by sending evil angels [among them]**.
>
> He made a way to his anger; he **spared not** their soul from death, but **gave their life over** to the pestilence;
>
> And smote all the firstborn in Egypt; the chief of [their] strength in the tabernacles of Ham. (Psalm 78:48–51, emphasis added)

So it was, in the case of Samson, that we are to read with the understanding that this narrative is within the setting of *permissive paradigm*. This paradigm was developed because of the decision of Israel to pick up the sword, to live by war and bloodshed—taking to themselves their own way of self-defense, securing God's promise by open aggression, operating in the mode of eye-for-eye retributive justice, and maintaining order by violent means. This environment paved the way by which Satan could readily capitalize upon his utmost in skill and cunning to make God look like the destroyer, *like himself*. In other words, he could pass off his own work as God's work. Remember, in all of this we are looking directly at the core of the conflict, as cited earlier:

> Jesus Christ is the Restorer. Satan, the apostate, is the destroyer. **Here is the conflict** between the Prince of life and the prince of this world, the power of darkness. (White, *Christ Triumphant*, p. 247, emphasis added)

We should understand that permissive paradigm was not functioning here in the same way as in the wars of Israel. There, God gave instructions *to humans* as to how *they* must employ the sword in order to ensure their survival. (God is not willing that any should perish but rather come to repentance.) God was not instructing Samson to do any of those acts. If it would have been so, it would also mean that God was sending holy angels to work out the feats of supernatural strength that were exhibited in the acts of Samson. This would be a false conclusion. *What permissive paradigm has to do with Samson is that it provided the environment in which Satan could find ready opportunity to sweep in a harvest of souls*. That is to say, under a belief system that holds God as a perpetrator of violence and bloodshed, Satan could find an entering wedge to influence a man like Samson—a special figure dedicated to God who was then corrupted in morals and principles— then work through him in a spectacular and supernatural way as though he were acting in accordance with the power of God. Such a situation is a perfect setup in which Satan can frame and defame God.

> Satan has control of all whom God does not especially guard.
> He will favor and prosper some, in order to further his own

designs, and he will bring trouble upon others and lead men to believe that it is God who is afflicting them. (White, *The Great Controversy*, p. 589)

I said previously that "God was not instructing Samson to do any of those acts." I meant to say this, in spite of the fact that it is written that the "spirit of the LORD came mightily upon him," and he tore a lion apart with his bare hands (Judges 14:5–6). This act later became the subject of a riddle posed for the Philistines (Judges 14:8–10, 12), and the outcome of Samson's vicious little game was that thirty men who attended Samson's marriage to a Philistine woman were torn to pieces by his own hands. It is astonishing language in Scripture, noting this otherwise forbidden marriage is written in inspiration as a divine ruse to get Samson into the Philistine territory so that he could spill their blood—his parents didn't know that this was "of the LORD" (Judges 14:4), and again, as the "spirit of the LORD came upon him," he killed thirty Philistines to get the garments promised in fulfillment of the deal for losing the riddle challenge (Judges 14:19). As it is said, *you can't make this up!*

The "Spirit of the Lord came mightily upon Samson" (*Signs of the Times*, Oct. 6, 1881, par. 10) as he burst the cords that bound him and proceeded to kill a thousand Philistines by bludgeoning them with the jawbone of a donkey, leaving them bloody and broken on the field with such lightning speed as to cause the enemy to flee in terror. Now, when Ellen White says, "The Spirit of the Lord," whether or not she understands the mechanism by which God "moved" Samson, we understand she writes in the same Hebraic mode as the Bible writers and was simply copying their use of the phrase. It was not, in fact, the Spirit of the Lord coming upon the person, but it was God standing aside and the spirit of Satan being let in.

Ellen White, even though taking great strides in giving us firm principles of interpretation for the strange acts of God and the understanding of biblical language, did not yet fully grasp the entire message or see the consistency of God's character "from A to Z." She was not given to make detailed applications of the principles to all the various stories of the Bible. She could not at that time give us the explanation of these things as it was not yet the time to develop them. We must remember the principles of inspiration as the mind of God *diffused* through the human mind and culture (White, Manuscript 243, 1886). Seeing things through a frosted glass can be interpreted as something other than what they truly are. Also, we must remember that reformation light is progressive, until the "the day dawn, and the day star arise" in our hearts (2 Peter 1:19).

So, coming back to Samson and the Spirit of the Lord, let's compare with some other passages that may give us clues. First, about Saul: "But the spirit of the LORD departed from Saul, and an evil spirit from the LORD troubled him" (1 Sam. 16:14). It would be that "an evil spirit from the LORD troubled" Samson in the same way, because the spirit of the LORD had departed from Samson also.

Second, concerning Jephthah:

> Then the spirit of the LORD came upon Jephthah ... And Jephthah vowed a vow unto the LORD, and said, If thou shalt without fail deliver the children of Ammon into mine hands, Then it shall be, that whatsoever cometh forth of the doors of my house to meet me, when I return in peace from the children of Ammon, shall surely be the LORD'S, and I will offer it up for a burnt offering. (Judges 11:29–31)

Well, it was his daughter who ended up being sacrificed. (Incidentally, we cannot interpret this as a human sacrifice in death; rather that she was dedicated to the Lord and to remain unmarried for life.) The point being made here is that a rash vow was apparently made under the Spirit of the LORD. Is this what God will inspire people to do?

Third, concerning Ahab:

> And the LORD said, Who shall persuade Ahab, that he may go up and fall at Ramothgilead? And one said on this manner, and

> another said on that manner. And there came forth a spirit, and stood before the LORD, and said, I will persuade him. And the LORD said unto him, Wherewith? And he said, I will go forth, and I will be a lying spirit in the mouth of all his prophets. And he said, Thou shalt persuade him, and prevail also: go forth, and do so. Now therefore, behold, the LORD hath put a lying spirit in the mouth of all these thy prophets, and the LORD hath spoken evil concerning thee. (1 Kings 22:20–23)

Note that the LORD put a lying spirit in control of the situation. This is biblical language and a reflection of the Hebrew mind. The belief was that God was responsible for everything, which in a sense is true because nothing happens that He does not allow. God allows evil to act because He cannot in righteousness completely restrain it without resorting to a violation of the principles of freedom and non-coercion. Therefore, it is said in human language that God put the lying spirit in the mouth of the prophets that convinced Ahab to go to battle. These spirits were not sent out by God as One who works in league with evil but rather this is biblical language *attributing to God the active position* when the way we would normally portray what actually happens is that the evil spirits demand access to those that are living by the rules of Satan's government and God, in righteousness and fairness, must give them that access because their subjects have chosen Satan's governing principles as their own; therefore, they have chosen Satan as their god.

We need to pay special attention to the phrase "the Spirit of the Lord came upon" in the text of the Samson narrative. The passages in Judges 14:5–6, 19, where Samson tore a young lion apart with his bare hands (establishing a prop that supported a chain of events that ended in the slaughter of thirty men of Ashkelon in order to loot their clothing to pay a debt), and in Judges 15:14, 15, where he broke his bonds and slew a thousand men, both employ the word *tsalach* [**H6713**], which, although translated in the King James Version as "came upon," is primarily translated in the Bible as "prosper." Young's Literal Translation of this verse renders it as "prospereth." God prospered him, allowed him to prevail and protect him throughout, even though it would not have been the modus operandi of Yahweh. It is more in keeping with the principles of Bible language that we would obtain this rendition of the word in this context, because God allowed His own purposes to prosper in the actions of Samson, even though Samson was functioning outside of God's character and methods, even under a spirit of carnal revenge. God allowed His own purpose for Samson to deliver Israel to *prosper*, even though Satanic motivations and actions would have prevailed in the life and errant ministry of Samson.

Samson also put himself under Satan's government and, if we could pull back the curtain, we would see that the spirits could have "come before the LORD," in figure and by eternal principle, to offer their services to fulfill the word of God to "begin to deliver Israel out of the hand of the Philistines" (Judges 13:5). This means, in objective effect, that Satan and his team would act to the full extent of the laws and restraints by which they must operate, that give them latitude to exercise both deception and force. (Is it dawning on us yet, what God is up against?) As God gave Samson over to the ruler that he had chosen, so also did He give the Philistines over to that same ruler. As Satan was given much latitude of operation on both sides, he could so orchestrate affairs as to achieve his purposes to denigrate the character of God and have it written down so that he could represent God as the author of violence while at the same time clap with glee in the bloodshed because in this he "gathers in his harvest" (*The Review and Herald*, September 17, 1901, par. 9).

So *am I saying* that, even though the Bible says that Samson's ways were of the LORD (Judges 14:4)—that his childish outbursts with their deadly consequences were effected under "the spirit of the LORD"—that they were actually NOT. This *is what I am saying* in one sense. In another sense, we have to say that these destructions *were* of the LORD because the language is to be interpreted in the modality of the hiding of face principle, wherein destruction occurs because God allows it, according to freedom of choice, and it is written as though God did it. We have a mandate to decode all things by valid principles of interpretation and a valid understanding of the nature of inspiration.

Additional Points to Ponder

Gifts of God

The idea has been posited that the statement "the gifts and calling of God are without repentance" (Rom. 11:29) would apply to Samson's supernatural strength. However, *we are not actually told that supernatural strength was part of the gift and calling of God to Samson*. The promise given, rather, was that he would "begin to deliver Israel out of the hand of the Philistines" (Judges 13:1–5, 19), and *this was fulfilled*.

Hair Power

How do we arrive at the principle that our vows will give us the strength to carry out God's will? Wasn't this a big deal with the mixed multitude that came out of Egypt to the giving of the law at Sinai? This is old covenant! Besides, where does the idea originate that his hair gave him his supernatural strength? Or why would we think that the prohibition against the use of the razor alone constituted the secret of his strength? Somehow the idea came in to trust in the symbol rather than in the Lord who gave the symbol. Sounds familiar, doesn't it?

The Nazarite Vow

The Nazarite vow also included a prohibition against consumption of alcoholic beverages. Samson broke this vow and yet still had strength. Where did Samson's strength come from? Ellen G. White says it became apparent, even as a child, "that he possessed extraordinary physical strength" (White, *Patriarchs and Prophets,* p. 562). His hair was not to be a cut as a sign of his consecration to God as a Nazarite, and his hair was a symbol of that consecration. The prohibition against the hair and the wine both served the same purpose, as did also the prohibition against eating unclean articles of food. Of his strength it is said that it was not "dependent upon his well-knit sinews, but upon his condition as a Nazarite, of which his unshorn hair was a symbol" (Ibid.). *Samson would have lost this gift of God when he broke the conditions*. (Do you understand the implication of this?) He had already indulged in the use of wine before we come to Delilah in the story. She was the woman from the valley of Sorek, "celebrated for its vineyards; these also had a temptation for the wavering Nazarite, who had already indulged in the use of wine, thus breaking another tie that bound him to purity and to God" (White, *Patriarchs and Prophets*, p. 565).

Samson "had transgressed the command of God by taking a wife from the Philistines" (White, *Patriarchs and Prophets*, p. 564). It is likely that this occurred very early on that he broke his Nazarite status not only through the use of wine but through his youthful forays into illegitimate "intimacies" with Philistine women. At this early point, as Samson rejected *his commitment to God, Satan took over the role of provider of strength to deceive Samson into thinking that the Lord was still giving him ability*.

We must interpret all the Bible narratives according to the principles of the righteousness of God as revealed in Jesus Christ and not according to what we think the Bible language is telling us.

Samson's Picture Hangs in the Hall of Faith

Why is that? One writer says, "Samson remains a hero of faith even though he killed many, because he is judged according to the cultural mindset he inherited and the terribly sorry state of Israel he was in" (Brown, *Reaching Samson,* p. 40). The inclusion of Samson in the list of Hebrews 11:32 seems out of place more than any of the other names. Here we have a puzzling attribution to Samson, along with others, of faith resulting in the fulfillment of God's promise to "subdue nations." Yet, as we examine the others, we find no lack of warts to blemish the faithful. We can ultimately include ourselves in this list. God winks at ignorance and saves us in situations in spite of ourselves. We must allow for this, knowing also that our knowledge of God has been incomplete. We will better reflect it in this time of the end as the Spirit of God is teaching us to look more fully at Christ and His representation of the character of God and how He does things. For example, Rahab is also in the list of Hebrews 11—a harlot who lied to protect God's servants. Elijah thought the right way was to cut up those idolaters. Certain of the disciples felt justified in calling for the incineration of inhospitable people.

We could provide many other examples of the faithful, who are not on this particular list.

Knowing what we know today, we cannot hold up these examples as models for our faith in every respect. Jesus must be our Model. Those who "keep the commandments and have the testimony of Jesus" are depicted as the final overcomers. They are the last reformers that hold the truth of God in a compromised world. These are the ones who have been perfected in knowledge, wisdom and grace. By God's grace, they have gone from glory to glory, faith to faith, maturing in their understanding and experience, until the "day star" has arisen in their hearts. They will be a witness even unto kings.

> Arise, shine; for thy light is come, and the glory of the LORD is risen upon thee. For, behold, the darkness shall cover the earth, and gross darkness the people: but the LORD shall arise upon thee, and his glory shall be seen upon thee. And the Gentiles shall come to thy light, and kings to the brightness of thy rising. (Isaiah 60:1–3)

A Plausible Etiology of Samson's Final Act

We should recognize that, through his demise, being blinded and thrust into prison, Samson came to repentance. This is the whole point of the Samson story, that he ended up in faith, even though he still engaged in mass slaughter. God's methods were not employed and Samson was working under the permissive paradigm, yet God's purposes were accomplished in it. Ostensibly, this would mean that Satan would be restricted in the work he could do through Samson. No longer would devil power bear sway in Samson's activities. So, what would have brought down the house?

I do not believe that a mere man, no matter how strong he might be physically, is a significant force upon a building made of stone. This requires physical assistance. How would Samson's strength be amplified without the involvement of angelic or demonic power?

"Harmonic resonance" could be a plausible solution. As Samson requests to be bound to the pillars of the pagan temple during a high feast to the god Dagon (see Judges 16:26), purposing in his heart to avenge himself on the Philistines, we find the reveling crowd on the rooftop swaying their bodies in synchronization to the "rock and roll" of the popular musicians of that time. As fate would have it, the tempo matched with the resonant frequency of the structure, which Samson recognized and utilized in applying rhythmic pressure to the pillars, much as we would rock a vehicle back and forth to free it from a stuck situation, keeping in rhythm with the natural rocking frequency of the vehicle. Or maybe his little bit of input at the bottom was not even a part of it—perhaps the temple might have come down solely by the doing of the Philistines.

What might we conclude from all this? Samson was morally weak and ignorant of God's ways, yet God turned the tables on Satan through all of that, accomplishing His purposes through Samson's independent actions and methods. We must be suspicious of that which we might call the moving of God and the power of God, ever examining our motives to see if those motives are actually in harmony with the glory of God, which is His character, and whether our methods truly characterize and exemplify *His methods* of bringing His plans to fruition. It is my belief that this particular time of ignorance is now past and that we have come to a time of repentance, finding our strength in His working, after the manner of Christ, in whom there was no violence (Acts 17:30; Isa. 53:9).

CHAPTER 12

Elijah, Elisha, and the Character of God

"Not by might, nor by power, but by my spirit, saith the LORD of hosts."
Zech.4:6

Did God instruct Elijah to slay the prophets of Ba'al? We'll get this out of the way right from the start. Yes. Further on in this period of history, the killing of God's enemies was to continue. "And it shall come to pass, that him that escapeth the sword of Hazael shall Jehu slay: and him that escapeth from the sword of Jehu shall Elisha slay" (1 Kings 19:17).

The ministries of the prophets Elijah and Elisha were carried out in times of permissive will, God's accommodations during the Old Testament times of ignorance which He winked at but now in the New Testament time He calls all of us to repentance (see Acts 17:30). Now we have seen Jesus, Emmanuel, so we know what God acts like (see 1 John 1:1–5).

As in many of the historical recounts of God giving instructions to kill the enemy for the purpose of their survival and deliverance, it was because this was *Israel's* chosen means, not the Lord's. He never intended that they should come to salvation by carnal warfare.

> Instead of pursuing the direct route to Canaan, which lay through the country of the Philistines, the Lord directed their course southward, toward the shores of the Red Sea. "For God said, Lest peradventure the people repent when they see war, and they return to Egypt." Had they attempted to pass through Philistia, their progress would have been opposed; for the Philistines, regarding them as slaves escaping from their masters, would not have hesitated to make war upon them. The Israelites were poorly prepared for an encounter with that powerful and warlike people. They had little knowledge of God and little faith in Him, and they would have become terrified and disheartened. They were unarmed and unaccustomed to war. (White, *Patriarchs and Prophets*, p. 282)

Josephus says that the wind and water currents washed the bodies and equipment up on the eastern side of the gulf and the weapons and armor were thus obtained in good supply. From there they sought to fight by conventional methods of human conquest and establish themselves in the land that God promised to them. Later, the testimony of the Spirit declared that the weapons that we are to use are not of human warfare, but of the Spirit of truth.

> For though we walk in the flesh, we do not war after the flesh: (For the weapons of our warfare [are] not carnal, but mighty through God to the pulling down of strong holds;) Casting down imaginations, and every high thing that exalteth itself against the knowledge of God, and bringing into captivity every thought to the obedience of Christ. (2 Corinthians 10:3–5)

> Earthly kingdoms rule by the ascendancy of physical power; but from Christ's kingdom every carnal weapon, every instrument of coercion, is banished. (White, *The Acts of the Apostles*, p. 12)

We need not delve any further into the lessons on permissive will here, nor the phenomenon of God giving instructions in the use of the sword.[14] Yet, it is useful to have a quick look at some incidents that took place while these men ministered the word of the Lord to His people. We can connect these incidents to the underlying realities of what really took place.

Elijah and the Curse of God

> **Earthly kingdoms rule by the ascendancy of physical power; but from Christ's kingdom every carnal weapon, every instrument of coercion, is banished.**

Elijah saw the condition of the people of God, how far they had sunk into apostasy. He prayed for the judgments of God to come and arrest them lest they should ultimately be utterly destroyed by their course of evil and idolatry. God did bring those judgments. He gave them up to their gods. He withdrew from them and from nature and drought came to the land, with no god to save.

> The time had come when God must speak to them by means of judgments. Inasmuch as the worshipers of Baal claimed that the treasures of heaven, the dew and the rain, came not from Jehovah, but from the ruling forces of nature, and that it was through the creative energy of the sun that the earth was enriched and made to bring forth abundantly, the curse of God was to rest heavily upon the polluted land. The apostate tribes of Israel were to be shown the folly of trusting to the power of Baal for temporal blessings. Until they should turn to God with repentance, and acknowledge Him as the source of all blessing, there

---

[14] Please refer to *As He Is* by 4th Angel Publications and volume one of *Awesome God* for coverage of the permissive paradigm.

> should fall upon the land neither dew nor rain. (White, *Prophets and Kings*, p. 120)

God's curse is not an arbitrary action. It is the simple outworking of cause and effect. They turned to Ba'al and the forces of nature, and God left them to their choice, which brought a curse instead of a blessing (see Deut. 31:16–18). We will come back to this point.

God's Messengers Are Blamed for Calamity

In the end-time scenario, the world will not recognize God's judgments aright. They will think that God is actively punishing, when the reality is that they have refused to acknowledge Him as the source of peace and blessing, so God gives them up and disaster befalls. As in the story of Elijah and the rulers of his time, blame is assigned to the people of God, for they have prophesied against the rebellious in their disobedience. The messengers are viewed as the ones bringing the trouble, when it is those who are disobedient and who are at fault, bringing their own wicked way back upon their heads.

> Jezebel utterly refused to recognize the drought as a judgment from Jehovah. Unyielding in her determination to defy the God of heaven, she, with nearly the whole of Israel, united in denouncing Elijah as the cause of all their misery. Had he not borne testimony against their forms of worship? If only he could be put out of the way, she argued, the anger of their gods would be appeased, and their troubles would end. (White, *Prophets and Kings*, p. 126)

> It is natural for the wrongdoer to hold the messengers of God responsible for the calamities that come as the sure result of a departure from the way of righteousness. Those who place themselves in Satan's power are unable to see things as God sees them. When the mirror of truth is held up before them, they

become indignant at the thought of receiving reproof. Blinded by sin, they refuse to repent; they feel that God's servants have turned against them and are worthy of severest censure. (White, *Prophets and Kings*, p. 139)

It is by the mighty power of the Infinite One that the elements of nature in earth and sea and sky are kept within bounds. And these elements He uses for the happiness of His creatures. "His good treasure" is freely expended "to give the rain ... in his season, and to bless all the work" of man's hands. Deuteronomy 28:12. (White, *Prophets and Kings*, p. 134)

The promise of abundance of rain had been given on condition of obedience. "It shall come to pass," the Lord had declared, "if ye shall hearken diligently unto My commandments which I command you this day, to love the Lord your God, and to serve Him with all your heart and with all your soul, that I will give you the rain of your land in his due season, the first rain and the latter rain, that thou mayest gather in thy corn, and thy wine, and thine oil. And I will send grass in thy fields for thy cattle, that thou mayest eat and be full.

"Take heed to yourselves," the Lord had admonished His people, "that your heart be not deceived, and ye turn aside, and serve other gods, and worship them; and then the Lord's wrath be kindled against you, and He shut up the heaven, that there be no rain, and that the land yield not her fruit; and lest ye perish quickly from off the good land which the Lord giveth you." Deuteronomy 11:10–17.

"If thou wilt not hearken unto the voice of the Lord thy God, to observe to do all His commandments and His statutes," the Israelites had been warned, "thy heaven that is over thy head shall be brass, and the earth that is under thee shall be iron. The Lord shall make the rain of thy land powder and dust: from heaven shall it come down upon thee, until thou be destroyed. Deuteronomy 28:15, 23, 24." (White, *Prophets and Kings*, p. 136)

The Heart of Elijah

Although Elijah is often thought of as a man of great zeal, which he was, and as one who was quick with the sword, I will speak in his defense. He lived in brutal times, under a different concept of deity than we now have. We can see in the lines of inspiration, however, that he had a heart for God's people, his own people. He lamented their condition and what would become of them were they not halted from their course.

> As Elijah saw Israel going deeper and deeper into idolatry, his soul was distressed and his indignation aroused. God had done great things for His people. He had delivered them from bondage and given them "the lands of the heathen ... that they might observe His statutes, and keep His laws.' Psalm 105:44, 45. But the beneficent designs of Jehovah were now well-nigh forgotten. Unbelief was fast separating the chosen nation from the Source of their strength. Viewing this apostasy from his mountain retreat, Elijah was overwhelmed with sorrow. In anguish of soul he besought God to arrest the once-favored people in their wicked course, to visit them with judgments, if need be, that they might be led to see in its true light their departure from Heaven. He longed to see them brought to repentance before they should go to such lengths in evil-doing as to provoke the Lord to destroy them utterly. (White, *Prophets and Kings*, p. 119)

Elijah Calls Fire on the Military Units

Ahaziah, son of Ahab, reigned over Israel after Ahab's death. He suffered a fall and was grievously wounded. He sent messengers to inquire of Baalzebub of Ekron if he should recover. Elijah sent messengers to intercept them, bringing the message from God to inquire why he should go to the god of Ekron when there was a living God to seek after? As a result, Elijah's men sent Ahaziah's men back with the message that he would perish. Ahaziah at once made determination that Elijah was the source of this message and dispatched a company to give a summons order to the prophet.

> Then the king sent unto him a captain of fifty with his fifty. And he went up to him: and, behold, he sat on the top of an hill. And he spake unto him, Thou man of God, the king hath said, Come down. And Elijah answered and said to the captain of fifty, If I be a man of God, then let fire come down from heaven, and consume thee and thy fifty. And there came down fire from heaven, and consumed him and his fifty. (2 Kings 1:9, 10)

Ahaziah thought then that by putting the arm on Elijah he could force the hand of God. The inspired pen gives us this context:

> **Anxious to avert, if possible, the threatened judgment**, he determined to send for the prophet. Twice Ahaziah sent a company of soldiers **to intimidate the prophet**, and twice the wrath of God fell upon them in judgment. The third company of soldiers humbled themselves before God; and their captain, as he approached the Lord's messenger, fell on his knees before Elijah, and besought him, and said unto him, O man of God, I pray thee, let my life, and the life of these fifty thy servants, be precious in thy sight. (White, *Prophets and Kings*, p. 208, emphasis added)

The ones who showed respect for the living God in this small gesture received again the presence and protection of God upon themselves, in spite of the king's haughty mission being carried out through them. God is merciful, not punishing.

If we were to see behind the curtain on these two incidents of the incineration of the first two companies, what would we see? Would God be charging up His flamethrower or would He be receding from His position of strength and protection? It is good to review here the principle revealed in *The Great Controversy* that explains, "Satan has control of all whom God does not especially guard. He will favor and prosper some, in order to further his own designs; and he will **bring trouble upon others and lead men to believe that it is God who is afflicting them**" (White, *The Great Controversy*, p. 589, emphasis added).

Another explanation is sometimes given, suggesting that God showed up in glory and no man can see God and live. When Christ declared Himself in the garden, the Roman soldiers fell back as dead men. The glory of the I AM knocked them over, but it did not kill them or burn them up. The third captain on his knees before Elijah said "Behold, there came fire down from heaven, and burnt up the two captains of the former fifties with their fifties" (2 Kings 1:14). Let us make a note here that this fire is not the same as the fire that God sent upon the altar at the showdown at Mt. Carmel. Unlike the fire upon the fifties, the fire that honored the sacrifice of Elijah was by the power of God. Satan had nothing to do with that. Satan could not interfere in this nor was he allowed to bring a false fire that would vindicate the prophets of Ba'al.

Later in his ministry, Elijah anoints Jehu, king of Israel, and Jehu goes to kill the house of Ahab and Jezebel, after the manner of the times.

> After he had been proclaimed king by the army, Jehu hastened to Jezreel, where he began his work of execution on those who had deliberately chosen to continue in sin and to lead others into sin. Jehoram of Israel, Ahaziah of Judah, and Jezebel the queen mother, with "all that remained of the house of Ahab in Jezreel, and all his great men, and his kinsfolks, and his priests," were slain. "All the prophets of Baal, all his servants, and all his priests" dwelling at the center of Baal worship near Samaria, were put to the sword. The idolatrous images were broken down

and burned, and the temple of Baal was laid in ruins. "Thus Jehu destroyed Baal out of Israel." 2 Kings 10:11, 19, 28. (White, *Prophets and Kings*, p. 215)

This is not what God wanted them to do any more than what He wants us to do. God does not change. In their faulty paradigm regarding how God functions, they became a threat against their enemies and God's enemies. God would release them upon those enemies when the latter had crossed the bounds of their protection, in the same manner as a whirlwind might fall upon them. He gave them over to the hand of His servants who exercised the sword under permissive will, which is God's accommodation to ignorance.

Hermeneutic Principles

We turn now to some important passages as interpretive guides to remind us of principles to apply to the reading of these Bible stories, and every story of God's judgments:

> I was shown that the judgments of God would not come directly out from the Lord upon them, but in this way: They place themselves beyond His protection. He warns, corrects, reproves, and points out the only path of safety; then if those who have been the objects of His special care will follow their own course independent of the Spirit of God, after repeated warnings, if they choose their own way, then He does not commission His angels to prevent Satan's decided attacks upon them. (White, *Manuscript Releases*, Vol. 14, p. 3)

These who pretend to be Christ's vicegerents upon earth do the works of their father the devil. **When did Christ leave them an example of putting to death either Romans or heathen because they did not believe His doctrines?**

> When John saw the insult put upon his Master in the deportment showing insult and contempt toward Jesus, he felt the wound for his Master, and asked: "Lord, wilt Thou that we command fire to come down from heaven, and consume them, even as Elias did?" Luke 9:54. Christ answered, "Ye know not what manner of spirit ye are of. For the Son of man is not come to destroy men's lives, but to save them." (White, Manuscript 62–Diary, Apr. 27, 1886, par. 63)
>
> Herod and the wicked authorities killed the Just One, but **Christ never killed anyone**, and we may attribute the spirit of persecution—because men want liberty of conscience—to its origin—Satan. He is a deceiver, a liar, a murderer, and accuser of the brethren. (Ibid., par. 64)

Remember that the disciples would not have been thinking of the fire upon the altar, but, in the words "consume them," they were referring to the fire that burned up the fifties.

In another place, focusing on the incident of the disciples desiring to burn up the enemies of God, we are informed that they were inspired by their recollection of Elijah's activity:

> Seeing Carmel in the distance, where Elijah slew the false prophets, they said, "Wilt thou that we command fire to come down from heaven, and consume them, even as Elias did?" They were surprised to see that Christ was pained by their words, and still more surprised as his rebuke fell upon their ears. (*The Review and Herald*, Feb. 7, 1899, par. 6)

In spite of Elijah's heart for his own people, that they might come to repentance, we may well ask if his spirit (and ours) might not be lacking with regard to the enemies of God and to God's people, our fellows? For some of us, it is easy to fall into the revenge trap.

> The rebuke given to James and John sounds down along the line to our time. Many reveal the attributes of Satan by trying to compel their fellow men to believe as they believe. They desire to punish those who, they think, dishonor Christ. They may say that they are working for truth and liberty, they may claim to be doing honor to God; but if they exercise a zeal that brings pain to the bodies and spirits of those who dare to differ with them, they are controlled by the enemy of God. Such may think themselves righteous; but Christ says to them, as to the disciples: "Ye know not what manner of spirit ye are of. For the Son of man is not come to destroy men's lives, but to save them." By his dealing with the Samaritans, Christ has shown us that although men manifest unmistakable contempt for him, his followers are not to harbor thoughts of hatred and revenge. (Ibid., par. 8)

The God that Answers by Fire or the Still Small Voice?

We have evidence that Elijah did not understand God's character and ways in the following passage that names him, along with John the Baptist, who had to be corrected, even as Elijah was corrected when he had fled to the desert in fear of Jezebel.

> Like the Saviour's disciples, John the Baptist did not understand the nature of Christ's kingdom …. He had looked for the high places of human pride and power to be cast down. He had pointed to the Messiah as the One whose fan was in His hand, and who would thoroughly purge His floor, who would gather the wheat into His garner, and burn up the chaff with unquenchable fire. Like the prophet Elijah, in whose spirit and power he had come to Israel, **he looked for the Lord to reveal Himself as a God that answereth by fire.** (White, *The Desire of Ages*, 215, emphasis added)

> The works of Christ not only declared Him to be the Messiah, but showed in what manner His kingdom was to be established. To John was opened the same truth that had come to Elijah in the desert, when "a great and strong wind rent the mountains, and brake in pieces the rocks before the Lord; but the Lord was not in the wind: and after the wind an earthquake; but the Lord was not in the earthquake: and after the earthquake a fire; but the Lord was not in the fire:" and after the fire, **God spoke to the prophet by "a still small voice."** 1 Kings 19:11, 12. So Jesus was to do His work, not with the clash of arms and the overturning of thrones and kingdoms, but through speaking to the hearts of men by a life of mercy and self-sacrifice. (White, *The Desire of Ages*, p. 217, emphasis added)

Later, Elisha succeeded Elijah in the prophetic office and ministry. Elisha functioned by the same paradigm.

Elisha Calls a Curse on the Mocking Youth

> At the sound of their mocking words the prophet turned back, and under the inspiration of the Almighty he pronounced a curse upon them. The awful judgment that followed was of God. "There came forth two she-bears out of the wood, and tare forty and two" of them. 2 Kings 2:23, 24. (White, *Prophets and Kings*, p. 235)

What does the pronouncement of a divine curse mean? Let us look at the first curse from God:

> And unto Adam he said, Because thou hast hearkened unto the voice of thy wife, and hast eaten of the tree, of which I commanded thee, saying, Thou shalt not eat of it: cursed is the

> ground for thy sake .... Thorns also and thistles shall it bring forth to thee. (Genesis 3:17, 18)

So, here again we have a view as to how God exercises power. Jesus later revealed who brought the thorns and thistles: "So the servants of the householder came and said unto him, Sir, didst not thou sow good seed in thy field? from whence then hath it tares? He said unto them, An enemy hath done this" (Matt. 13:27, 28).

God shows His power by withdrawing it. Its effects are felt when it is not there. We do not pay attention to the lack of pain or poverty nearly as much as we do to their presence. This is a call to constant gratitude for all our blessings. When He who reads the heart makes the determination that He can no longer exercise His grace, He must hide His face. Restraints are loosened on wickedness and/or the protective, sustaining guidance of the forces of the natural realm is taken away. Then the destroyer can exercise his power and lead men to believe that God is doing it.

Yet even the child, as he comes in contact with nature, will see cause for perplexity. He cannot but recognize the working of antagonistic forces. It is here that nature needs an interpreter. Looking upon the evil manifest even in the natural world, all have the same sorrowful lesson to learn—"An enemy hath done this" (Matt. 13:28).

Only in the light that shines from Calvary can nature's teaching be read aright. Through the story of Bethlehem and the cross let it be shown *how* good is to conquer evil, and *how* every blessing that comes to us is a gift of redemption.

> In brier and thorn, in thistle and tare, is represented the evil that blights and mars. In singing bird and opening blossom, in rain and sunshine, in summer breeze and gentle dew, in ten thousand objects in nature, from the oak of the forest to the violet that blossoms at its root, is seen the love that restores. And nature still speaks to us of God's goodness. (White, *Education*, p. 101)

Satan is always the destroyer and God is always the Restorer. Satan likes to trick people into believing the reverse through bringing destruction or false blessings. Whether Elisha would have understood these things or not—most likely not—he was yet under permissive will in Israel, and he was inspired to call the curse of God upon them according to his understanding and God let it come according to the reality of how He uses power. The Lord's hand being removed, the enemy would bring the bears to attack the youth, leaving an impression that God acts like this.

Likewise, later, in 2 Kings, Chapter 5, we have the story of Elisha working to bring God's healing in response to the faith exhibited by the leprous Syrian captain, Naaman. We read about Elisha's servant Gehazi scheming to enrich himself and, in so doing, bringing disrepute upon God and Elisha. This brought from Elisha the pronouncement that Naaman's leprosy would fall upon his lying servant. Here we can see that God, who knows all things, would have inspired Elisha to call the manner of calamity that would befall this one who had apparently reached the point of disconnect from God and His power. God did not bring the disease. He pronounced the species of consequence that would ensue from losing His protection.

It is all about reaping and sowing. We pray earnestly that we cultivate the right relationship with God, placing our hand firmly in His, every day until we take our last breath. God is good, all the time.

Bibliography

Brown, Danutsan. *Reaching Samson.* Maranatha Media, 2020.

Clute, Michael F. *Into the Father's Heart.* Woodburn, OR: God's Last Call Ministries, 2005.

"Community Health & Restorative Practices, Reports and Recommendations." International Institute for Restorative Practices, https://1ref.us/stra2 (accessed Dec. 7, 2022).

"Constantinian Shift." Wikipedia. https://1ref.us/stra3 (accessed Aug. 5, 2021).

Guantánamo Bay: 14 Years of Injustice. Amnesty International UK, 2019.

Alonzo T. Jones, "Society and the State, or the Origin of Civil Governments," *The Bible Echo*, Melbourne, Australia: Echo Publishing Company Limited, Vol. 12, No. 39, July 26, 1897, p. 236.

Jones, A.T. "The Third Angel's Message." *General Conference Bulletin,* Volume 1, 1895:

———. "Through the Bible—IV." *The Medical Missionary Articles (1903–1909),* April 15, 1908.

Josephus, Flavius. *Antiquities of the Jews,* Book X. Chicago: University of Chicago, https://1ref.us/stra7 (accessed Nov. 30, 2022).

Lohnes, Kate. "Siege of Jerusalem: Jewish-Roman War." (accessed Aug. 5, 2021).

Shen, Michael Li-Tek. *Canaan to Corinth: Paul's Doctrine of God and the Issue of Food Offered to Idols in 1 Corinthians 8:1–11:1.* New York: Peter Lang Publishing, Inc., 2010.

South African Truth and Reconciliation Commission. https://1ref.us/stra1 (accessed July 31, 2021).

Straub, Kevin. *Awesome God: Songs of His Power, Volume 1.* TEACH Services, Inc.: Calhoun, GA, 2022.

"The Supernatural Gift of Understanding Foreign and ancient Languages." Miracles of the Saints, https://1ref.us/stra6 (accessed Dec. 6, 2022).

"Tyndale Bible." Wikipedia. https://1ref.us/stra5 (accessed Nov. 30, 2022).

Tyndale, William. *Doctrinal Treatises and Introduction to Different Portions of the Holy Scriptures.* Australia: Wentworth Press, 2019.

———. *The Obedience of a Christian Man.* New York: Penguin Books, 2000.

Waggoner, E.J. *The Everlasting Covenant.* London: International Tract Society, Limited, 1900.

———. "The Reign of Peace." *The Signs of the Times,* Vol. 19, Oct. 9, 1893.

———. "A Wise Answer." *The Present Truth* [UK], Apr. 19, 1894.

Waite, Arthur E. *A New Encyclopedia of Freemasonry and of Cognate Instituted Mysteries: Their Rites, Literature and History*, Volume I. Weathervane Books, 1970.

White, Ellen G. "A Time of Trouble." *Review and Herald*, Sept. 17, 1901.

———. *The Acts of the Apostles*. Mountain View, CA: Pacific Press Publishing Association, 1911.

———. *The Adventist Home.* Hagerstown, MD: Review and Herald Publishing Association, 1952.

———. "Christ and the Law." *Signs of the Times*, Apr. 14, 1898.

———. "Christ Our Hope." *Review and Herald*, Dec. 20, 1892.

———. *Christ Triumphant.* Hagerstown, MD: Review and Herald Publishing Association, 1999.

———. "Co-Laborers with Christ." *Review and Herald*, Mar. 8, 1887.

———. *Confrontation*. Washington, DC: Review and Herald Publishing Association, 1971.

———. *Counsels on Health.* Mountain View, CA: Pacific Press Publishing Association, 1923.

———. *Counsels to Parents, Teachers, and Students.* Mountain View, CA: Pacific Press Publishing Association, 1913.

———. "Danger in Rejecting Light." *The Review and Herald*, October 21, 1890.

———. *The Desire of Ages*. Mountain View, CA: Pacific Press Publishing Association, 1898.

———. *Early Writings*. Washington, DC: Review and Herald Publishing Association, 1882.

———. *Education*. Mountain View, CA: Pacific Press Publishing Association, 1903.

———. *The Ellen G. White 1888 Materials*. Washington, DC: Ellen G. White Estate, 1987.

———. *Fundamentals of Christian Education*. Nashville, TN: Southern Publishing Association, 1923.

———. "God's Desire for His People." *Review and Herald*, Aug. 26, 1909.

———. "God's Word Our Study-Book." *The Youth's Instructor*, June 30, 1898.

———. *Gospel Workers*. Washington, DC: Review and Herald Publishing Association, 1915.

———. *The Great Controversy*. Mountain View, CA: Pacific Press Publishing Association, 1911.

———. *Heaven*. Nampa, ID: Pacific Press Publishing Association, 2003.

———. "Knowing Christ." *Signs of the Times*, Jan. 27, 1898.

———. Letter 244. July 17, 1906.

———. *Letters and Manuscript—Volume 4 (1883–1886)*. Ellen G. White Estate, 1886.

———. *Letters and Manuscript—Volume 11 (1896)*. Ellen G. White Estate, 1896.

———. *Letters and Manuscript—Volume 14 (1899)*. Ellen G. White Estate, 1899.

———. *Manuscript Releases*. Vol. 6. Silver Spring, MD: Ellen G. White Estate, 1990.

———. *Manuscript Releases*. Vol. 14. Silver Spring, MD: Ellen G. White Estate, 1990.

———. *Manuscript Releases*. Vol. 16. Silver Spring, MD: Ellen G. White Estate, 1990.

———. *Manuscript Releases*. Vol. 21. Silver Spring, MD: Ellen G. White Estate, 1993.

———. *Patriarchs and Prophets*. Washington, DC: Review and Herald Publishing Association, 1890.

———. *Prophets and Kings*. Mountain View, CA: Pacific Press Publishing Association, 1917.

———. "Redemption–No. 1." *Review and Herald*, Feb. 24, 1874.

———. *The Review and Herald*, Feb. 7, 1899.

———. *The Review and Herald*, September 17, 1901.

———. *Review and Herald*, May 10, 1906.

———. *The SDA Bible Commentary*. Vol. 2. Washington, DC: Review and Herald Publishing Association, 1953.

———. *The SDA Bible Commentary*. Vol. 4. Washington, DC: Review and Herald Publishing Association, 1955.

———. *The SDA Bible Commentary*. Vol. 6. Washington, DC: Review and Herald Publishing Association, 1956.

———. *Selected Messages*. Book 2. Washington, DC: Review and Herald Publishing Association, 1958.

———. *Signs of the Times*, Oct. 6, 1881.

———. *The Spirit of Prophecy*. Vol. 1. Battle Creek, MI: Seventh-day Adventist Publishing Association, 1870.

———. *The Spirit of Prophecy*. Vol. 4. Battle Creek, MI: Seventh-day Adventist Publishing Association, 1884.

———. *Spiritual Gifts*. Vol. 1. Battle Creek, MI: Seventh-day Adventist Publishing Association, 1858.

———. *Steps to Christ*. Mountain View, CA: Pacific Press Publishing Association, 1892.

———. *Testimonies for the Church*. Vol. 1. Mountain View, CA: Pacific Press Publishing Association, 1868.

———. *Testimonies for the Church*. Vol. 5. Mountain View, CA: Pacific Press Publishing Association, 1889.

———. *Testimonies to Ministers and Gospel Workers*. Mountain View, CA: Pacific Press Publishing Association, 1923.

———. "Words to the Young." *The Youth's Instructor*, Nov. 30, 1893.

Yoder, John H. *Christian Attitudes to War, Peace, and Revolution*. Grand Rapids, MI: The Institute of Mennonite Studies, Brazos Press, 2009.

TEACH Services, Inc.
PUBLISHING
www.TEACHServices.com • (800) 367-1844

We invite you to view the complete
selection of titles we publish at:
www.TEACHServices.com

We encourage you to write us
with your thoughts about this,
or any other book we publish at:
info@TEACHServices.com

TEACH Services' titles may be purchased in
bulk quantities for educational, fund-raising,
business, or promotional use.
bulksales@TEACHServices.com

Finally, if you are interested in seeing
your own book in print, please contact us at:
publishing@TEACHServices.com

We are happy to review your manuscript at no charge.

www.ingramcontent.com/pod-product-compliance
Lightning Source LLC
Chambersburg PA
CBHW070357240426
43671CB00013BA/2540